T0018111

ALL
TOGETHER
NOW

By The Same Author

OLD WINE IN A NEW BOTTLE
MAGIC ACES
OUT OF THE BOX

ALL
TOGETHER
NOW

A COLLECTION OF AMAZING CARD TRICKS

ALL YOU NEED
TO KNOW

Stuart Lee

ISBN: 978-1-4669-1965-5 (sc)
ISBN: 978-1-4669-1964-8 (e)

Trafford rev. 12/16/2013

 www.trafford.com

North America & international
toll-free: 1 888 232 4444 (USA & Canada)
fax: 812 355 4082

Contents

INTRODUCTION

ALTHOUGH AT A VERY young age, like most other children, I had been delighted and intrigued by so-called "magic" tricks, particularly those involving playing cards, at no time had I shown anything more than a passing interest in performing them myself. However, as the years went by, having witnessed a particularly striking performance of a trick, I would be sufficiently enthused to find out how it had been done. Thus, over time, I acquired the ability to perform a few very simple tricks with an ordinary pack of cards and some more impressive ones with the aid of specially prepared packs.

On some high days and holidays, I could be encouraged by friends to show off one or more of these tricks. They were a most accommodating audience. In fact, I suspect that on most occasions they were as aware as I was of how the effect was being achieved. Nevertheless, a trick (however simple) is always intriguing and they encouraged me.

What converted this spasmodic and moderate interest in card magic into an almost all-consuming pursuit was a combination of circumstances some ten Christmases ago. I had retired from a long career in the Army some years before and therefore I then had the time and opportunity to indulge all my hobbies and interests. On that particular Christmas my wife and I were staying in Northumberland with my wife's sister and her husband and to keep me amused they presented me with a book of puzzles, games and tricks. The contents more than lived up to the title: "*The Curious Book of Mind-Boggling Tricks, Puzzles and Games*" (Charles Barry Townsend, Sterling Publishing Co. Inc., New York). Although the puzzles and games certainly kept me amused, it was the card tricks that particularly attracted my attention. Most of them I had already come across before in one form or another but some of them were new to me. In any event, I had the time over the Christmas holiday to give to each of them a little more attention than I had when I had come across them before. The result was that I spent that Christmas and a few weeks after it pondering on how they might be developed and improved.

While doing so I began to search my local lending libraries and bookshops for anything I could find on card magic and it soon became apparent from the references and bibliographies that I found in the books I came across that there was a wealth of material available. I determined therefore to acquire a basic reference library that would enable me to become acquainted with a whole spectrum of card tricks and routines and the skills and sleights-of-hand associated with them. As it might spare the reader many hours of searching out such books for him- or herself the results of my forays in the bookshops are set out here.

The first acquisition was "*The Royal Road to Card Magic*" by Jean Hugard and Frederick Braué (Dover Publications

Inc., New York, 1999), which proved to be a most useful introduction to a range of basic card manipulations and tricks involving these skills. This was followed by the book "*Expert Card Technique*" (Dover Publications Inc., New York, 1974) by the same authors, which guides the reader through more complicated techniques and effects. Next Hugard's "*Encyclopaedia of Card Tricks*" (Dover Publications Inc., New York, 1974 and Foulsham, Slough, 2003) proved to be a veritable cornucopia of information not only on the card tricks themselves but also of the underlying principles and specialist and pre-prepared packs. It also includes a brief guide to the performance of a number of basic sleights-of-hand and a description of "*The Nikola Card System*" for memorising the order of the cards in a pack.

These three books alone were more than enough to satisfy my requirements for a basic reference library, but, as with most interests, the more I studied them the more I wanted more information on particular aspects of card magic. The first was the ways in which the principles of mathematics could be applied to handling and ordering the cards. Again, I found that there was no lack of material, but there were two books that particularly attracted my attention: Arthur F. MacTier's "*Card Concepts*" (Davenport, London, 2000) and Martin Gardner's "*Mathematics, Magic, and Mystery*" (Dover Publications Inc., New York, 1956). The former is a most comprehensive review of what the author describes in the book's subtitle as the "numerical and sequential principles within card magic". It also gives detailed descriptions of tricks with cards using these principles. Finally, it provides a wealth of information on other authors, sources, and references in the field. Martin Gardner's book describes not only tricks with cards but also a variety of other effects that can be produced by applying mathematical principles.

The second area of card magic that attracted my particular attention was that of the systems that could be used to memorise the order of the cards in a pre-arranged pack. "*The Nikola Card System*" referred to above is one, but there are many more. Juan Tamariz's book "*Mnemonica*" (Hermetic Press Inc., Seattle, 2004), although concentrating on his own "ultra-rapid" system and the many effects that can be produced from it, also describes and gives references for most of the other systems that have been developed, eg "The Rosary Deck", "The Eight Kings System", "The Si Stebbins Stack", etc. However, after much research and personal experimentation, the system I found to be the most suited to my purposes and also easy to master was that set out in the book "*The Osterlind Breakthrough Card System*" (Osterlind Mysteries, 2004) by Richard Osterlind. Although this system is not designed to allow you to memorise the order of the cards in the pre-arranged pack it does allow you immediately to identify any given card from the identity of either the preceding or following card in the pack.

My next area of interest was those tricks in card magic described as "self-working". I soon found that one author in particular, Karl Fulves, had concentrated his attention on such tricks and his books (all published by Dover Publications Inc., New York) were added to my ever-growing library: "*Self-Working Card Tricks*" (1974), "*More Self-Working Card Tricks*" (1984), "*Self-Working Close-Up Card Magic*" (1995) and, for the card tricks included, "*Self-Working Mental Magic*" (1979).

Having collected together all this material I settled down to study it. I worked through the descriptions of the tricks and noted those that produced the most spectacular effects. I amended them, where it seemed appropriate, and, in some cases, using the principles involved in one trick I developed another with what I considered to be a more impressive outcome. I practised the sleights-of-hand and, where I could, simplified and, hopefully, improved the handling of the cards. Finally, I began to put together sequences of tricks into routines that allowed one trick to follow naturally from and build on the trick that preceded it.

It was at this point that I came to the conclusion that what would help me to remember the tricks and allow me to present them in the most effective way was a carefully thought-through structured sequence of routines set out in a note-book that I could use to give me an overview of the sequences and allow me, from time to time, to refresh my memory on the handling and presentation of a particular trick. Once completed I found it an indispensable tool in learning and retaining the mechanics of the tricks and it occurred to me that with some additional background information it could prove to be as useful to others as it was for me. On this basis I produced my first book on card magic "*Old Wine In A New Bottle*" (Trafford, Bloomington, 2010). My aim was to produce a practical hand-book that would guide the beginner in card magic through the basic handling of the cards to the successful production of the tricks. I included in it not only detailed descriptions of the working of the tricks but also advice on presentation and full explanations of the techniques that can be used to manipulate and control the cards. All this was set in the context of a routine based on "classic" tricks reworked to produce sometimes new, sometimes stronger, outcomes.

I followed this with a second book "*Magic Aces*" (Trafford, Bloomington, 2011) which, in addition to the basic information on the handling and manipulation of the cards, sets out a routine of tricks in which the Aces of the pack are produced in a variety of novel and spectacular ways. My third book, "*Out of The Box*" (Trafford, Bloomington,

2012) followed the same formula, based on a routine of tricks performed with the cards taken straight from the sealed carton.

It is on these three books that this book is based.

All the tricks can be performed using the minimum manipulation of the cards and, although variations of the tricks using sleights-of-hand are described, they can be performed without them and detailed instructions for such performance are set out.

In the books "*Old Wine In A New Bottle*", "*Magic Aces*" and "*Out of The Box*" it was necessary to begin with definitions of the terms used in describing the cards and in describing the handling of the cards. These are set out below.

All 52 cards together are *the pack* or *the deck*

Any part of the pack is *a packet*

A hand (of cards) is a packet that has been dealt to or given to a spectator

To deal consecutively is to deliver to each hand in turn one card until the deal is completed. *To deal the hands individually* is to deliver all the cards required to one hand before proceeding to deal the next hand.

To count cards reversing their order is to place each card as it is counted on top of the previous card. *To count cards without reversing their order* is to place each card as it is counted beneath the previous card.

Face-down and *face-up* cards are self-evident terms, the face of a card being its value and suit.

The long edge of a card, packet, or pack is *the side*.

The short edge of a card, packet, or pack is *the end*.

Front and *forward* and *outward* are away from you, and *rear* and *backward* and *inward* are towards you.

Left and *right* are from your viewpoint.

With the end of the cards or pack pointing towards the spectators, *the outer end* is the end pointing towards the spectators, and *the inner end* is the end pointing towards you.

With the cards or pack held in the right hand and with the outer end pointing towards the spectators, the outer side is to the right and the inner side is towards the left. Similarly, if the outer side is pointing towards the spectators the outer end is to the right and the inner end is to the left.

With the cards or pack held in the left hand and the outer end pointing towards the spectators the outer side is to the left and the inner side is to the right. Similarly, if the outer side is pointing towards the spectators the outer end is to the left and the inner end is to the right.

The fingers are: *first* (or *index*), *second*, *third* (or *ring*), and *fourth* (or *little*, sometimes referred to as "*the pinky*").

To cut and complete is to take a packet of cards from the top of the pack and to place what was the bottom of the pack on top of it. With the cards in hand the same outcome is achieved by *the undercut*, where the bottom part of the pack is cut away and transferred to the top of the pack.

To cull is to extract a card or cards (either openly or secretly) from the rest of the cards in a pack or packet.

An *out-jogged* or *up-jogged* card or packet is a card or packet positioned in the pack so that the card or packet projects from the pack.

A break is a small gap or opening formed secretly within a packet or pack at either the inner end or at the inner corner of the inner side. The former is held by the tip of the thumb of the hand holding the cards and the latter by the tip of the little finger of the hand holding the cards (and for this reason it is sometimes referred to as "*a pinky break*").

A bridged card is a card that has been subjected to pressure either at the sides or the ends to produce a curve along its length or across its width. A forward curve to the face of a card is a *convex bridge*, and a rearward curve to the face of a card is a *concave bridge*.

A few concluding words of advice for the beginner in card magic:

Study the descriptions of the handling and presentation carefully before you attempt to perform them.

Go through the manipulations and presentation slowly on the first attempts.

Try not to look at your hands when shuffling or performing a manipulation.

Perform the manipulations and presentations over and over again in practice and perform a trick for others only when you are totally confident of your ability to do so successfully.

If necessary, distract the attention of the spectators away from the cards by diverting their attention elsewhere. This can be done by talking to them directly and requiring a response or by giving them something to do or to look at.

Do not be afraid when the occasion requires it to perform some manipulations openly. It is surprising what can go unnoticed provided it is done boldly and the attention of the spectators distracted by directing it elsewhere.

When you are performing a trick do not rush the presentation. You know the trick and the effect you are attempting, but, hopefully, it is the first time the spectators have seen the trick performed and to rush the presentation would be to confuse them.

As a general rule, never repeat a trick in the same performance. Exceptions are where the same effect or outcome can be achieved by different means or when the mechanics of the trick are such that it is impossible for the spectators to determine how the effect is brought about.

And **never ever** reveal how an effect has been achieved.

THE CARDS

IT MIGHT WELL BE said that performers of card magic are spoiled for choice by the variety of playing cards available to them. There are giant-sized cards and miniature cards, triangular cards, and circular cards. They have plain backs in a full spectrum of colours or patterned backs in as many styles and designs as there are manufacturers. However, the majority of performers prefer to use either the *"Poker-size"* card or the *"Bridge-size"* card, the former being the larger of the two sizes.

A popular example of the Poker-size pack of cards is the *"Bicycle Rider Back"* pack produced by the U.S. Playing Card Co. It has two indexes on the face of each card (ie, the value and suit of each card are shown at the top left and at the bottom right corners) and it can be obtained in a variety of colours for the backs. Of particular interest to some performers is the fact that the packs can also be obtained with blank-faced, blank-backed, double-faced, double-backed cards, and in a miniature size with red, black or green backs in a design identical to the full-size packs. Additionally, they are available as specially prepared packs to perform particular tricks and effects.

Examples of the Bridge-size packs are the "*No 1*" pack of the Waddington Playing Card Co. Ltd. (Winning Moves UK Ltd.) and the "*Standard*" playing cards produced and sold by W.H. Smith. They come either Red-backed or Blue-backed and are four-indexed cards with the value and suit of the cards shown at all four corners of each card. Waddington also produce a four-indexed "*No 1*" Poker pack. An advantage of a four-indexed pack is that irrespective of whether the face of the pack is fanned or spread from left to right or right to left the indexes of the cards are equally visible. Additionally, some performers find the smaller Bridge-size cards easier to handle.

For completeness it should be noted that W.H. Smith produce and sell miniature "*Patience*" packs in identical back design and colour to their "*Standard*" packs and also a Poker-size pack—this latter pack being a card with two extra-large indexes on the face of the card.

A fourth range of playing cards merits attention and that is the "*Classic*" design produced by the Austrian company Piatnik. They are Bridge-size cards available in back designs in red and blue and also in special packs (ie, blank backs, blank faces, etc.). However, because of their order in the sealed pack they are not suitable for use in the routine described in the chapter "*Out of The Box*". It should also be noted that the descriptions of the handling set out in that chapter assume the use of the "*Bicycle Rider Back*" pack. The handling required for the Waddington "*No 1*" pack and the W.H. Smith "*Standard*" pack are given in the section on alternative packs in that chapter.

"MAGIC ACES"

I N CARD MAGIC THE TRICKS involving the use of the Aces have always been foremost among those that impress spectators.

Try an experiment on yourself or a spectator. Deal out face-up onto a table four cards, including one Ace. Immediately, turn all the cards face-down. Which card stood out from the others? It was, of course, the Ace.

A King, a Queen, and a Jack are certainly more colourful than the Aces, and they and all the other cards of the pack have more detail on them than an Ace, but it is the Aces that create the strongest impression. They are easily recognised and remembered by a spectator, who is always intrigued when one or more of them is produced from the pack in a surprising way. There are many reasons for this: as the Aces have the least detail on them than any of the cards in the pack they have the strongest visual impact; in almost all card games they are the winning card or they are the cards that are used to form the winning hand; they are the only cards that in some card games can have a high or a low value depending on the requirement of the hand; in many fields of endeavour "an Ace" is the best there is; and in tennis "an Ace" is an un-playable first serve. Given all these attributes and associations it is little wonder that the Aces command the immediate attention of the spectator.

This chapter sets out complete instructions for the performance of a routine of card tricks—all of them involving effects based on the revelation of the Aces in a variety of surprising ways.

Very little skill in card manipulation is required to perform the routine and any manipulations that are required are fully explained and described in the chapter "*Handling and Sleights-of-Hand*". With regard to the sleights-of-hand the routine can be performed without the use of any as the tricks are self-working—the sleights-of-hand being used, in almost all cases, only to create the illusion that the cards are being indiscriminately mixed.

The whole routine lasts for approximately 25-30 minutes.

Preparation

To perform the routine you require two packs of cards of identical design but with different coloured backs, eg, one blue, one red.

With regard to your choice of packs you should note that the "*Bicycle Rider Back*" packs and the W.H. Smith cards are readily available in a "miniature" or approximately half-sized pack with back designs and colour identical to the full-sized packs. These packs can be used to strengthen the presentation of one of the tricks in the routine ("*Telepathic Aces*") although the trick can be performed using only the full-sized packs.

You should also note that whatever packs you decide to use for the routine you will need four Joker cards for each pack to perform the trick "*You Must Be Joking*" and you will therefore need to purchase two packs of each back colour.

Having decided on your choice of packs the two packs required for the routine should be ordered (or "*stacked*") in preparation for the first tricks of the routine ("*Finding The Aces*" and "*You Must Be Joking*"). Obviously, if such preparation is not possible then these two tricks cannot be performed. They should be replaced by tricks from the section of this chapter giving adaptations and alternatives.

To prepare the packs you should begin by extracting the Joker cards and any extraneous cards from the packs. Discard the extraneous cards (eg. scoring-cards, promotional cards, etc) and place the Blue-backed Jokers with the Blue-backed pack and the Red-backed Jokers with the Red-backed pack.

You now arrange (or stack) the packs for the routine as follows:

a. First take the Blue-backed pack and order the face-down pack as follows:
   (*Top*): Red Ace – the 4 Jokers – any 11 cards – Black Ace – any 18 cards – Black Ace – any 9 cards – Red Ace – any 9 cards and the bridged card (or any 10 cards if you are not using a bridged card).
   (*For an explanation on how to prepare and use a bridged card see the relevant section in the chapter on "Handling and Sleights-of-Hand".*)
b. Place the pack in the appropriate carton.
c. Now take the Red-backed pack and order the face-down pack in exactly the same way.

An alternative method of ordering the pack, which is easier to recall from memory, is to extract the Aces from the pack and to proceed as follows: in the face-down pack place an Ace at the following positions: 12th card, 31st card, and 41st card. Then place the four Joker cards face-down on top of the pack and the final Ace face-down on top of the Jokers. If you are using a bridged card ensure that this card is the bottom card of the arranged pack.

With the packs so arranged you are now ready to perform the routine of tricks.

The Routine

1. Begin with the two prepared packs of cards in their cartons on the table.
2. The spectator or spectators are asked to choose which pack they wish you to use. Take this pack out of its carton, taking care not to disturb the pre-arranged order of the cards.
3. If you are not using a bridged card proceed directly to paragraph 4 below. If you are using a bridged card you may now perform "a false mix of the pack" or you may, if you wish, merely allow the spectator to "cut and complete" the pack before you finally cut the bridged card to the bottom of the pack. *(For an explanation of how to perform "a false mix of the pack" and how to use the bridged card see the relevant sections in the chapter on "Handling and Sleights-of-Hand".)*
4. Turn the pack face-up and spread out the cards to show the mix, taking care not to display the bottom five cards of the face-up pack, which are the four Jokers and an Ace. Once the pack has been displayed turn it face-down and place it on the table.
5. Explain that as all the tricks you are going to perform involve the "Magic Aces" you will need a little help to find them.

First Trick:
"Finding The Aces"

The performer seeks the assistance of the spectator or spectators to find the Aces in a face-down pack. The first Ace is discovered by the spectator cutting off half the pack and dealing off the cards to an apparently arbitrarily chosen number. The second Ace is discovered by the spectator choosing a number between 10 and 20 and again dealing off cards from a packet to a card arrived at in the same arbitrary way. The third Ace is discovered using any number chosen between 20 and 30. The performer produces the fourth Ace from the bottom of the pack.

PERFORMANCE

1. Challenge a spectator to cut off exactly half of the pack from the top of the face-down pack and, when he or she has done so, to hand it to you. To confirm that it is half of the pack deal the cards out face-down into a pile on the table, counting them out aloud as you do so (*you are, in fact, also reversing their order*). If there are 26 cards congratulate the spectator on the accuracy of his or her cut. If there are more than 26 cards stop the deal at 26 and return the extra cards face-down to the top of the rest of the pack without disturbing their order. If you have less than 26 cards make the total up to 26 by taking cards in turn off the top of the rest of the

pack and placing them face-down in turn on the top of the pile of counted cards.

2. Take the face-down pile of cards you have counted out and neaten them up. You then challenge the spectator again to cut the pile exactly in half. When he or she has done so count out the cards. If there are 13 cards, congratulate the spectator. If there are 10 or more merely comment on this. If there are less than 10 make up the number to any number the spectator chooses above 10 by taking the necessary number off the top of the pile. Then take the remaining cards and place them aside.

3. Now instruct the spectator to take the number of cards arrived at and to add the two digits together to give a single digit number (ie. 14 = 1 + 4 = 5). The spectator then takes the pile of cards from the table, counts down in the pile to the card at that number and then takes the card at that position in the pile. (*It will be an Ace.*) Place the card face-up on the table.

4. Take all the other cards of the pile from which the spectator has been counting and place them all face-down on top of the cards you placed aside at paragraph 2 above. Then pick up this consolidated pile of cards and place them **beneath** the other half of the pack.
    (*NOTE: If these moves have been correctly performed the bottom cards of the face-down pack are now the four Joker cards and an Ace.*)

5. You now invite the spectator to think of and state any number he or she wishes between 10 and 20. When he or she has done so deal off face-down from the top of the face-down pack that number of cards into a face-down pile. Take the two digits of the number he or she gave and add them together to give a single digit number. The spectator then takes the pile of cards,

counts down to that number, and takes the card at that position. (*It will be an Ace.*) Place it face-up by the side of the other Ace.

6. Take all the other cards and place them face-down **on top** of the rest of the face-down pack.

7. Next invite the spectator to think of and state any number her or she wishes between 20 and 30 and for that number repeat the procedure described at paragraph 5 above. (*The spectator will arrive at the third Ace.*) Place it face-up by the side of the other Aces and place all the other cards face-down on top of the rest of the face-down pack.

8. Remark that all you need now is the fourth and final Ace—and, as you are doing so, take the bottom card of the pack and place it face-down by the side of the three face-up Aces. Instruct the spectator to turn the card face-up. (*When he or she does so it will be the fourth Ace.*)

Second Trick:
"You Must Be Joking"

Effect

After placing the four Aces face-down on the face-down pack the spectator cuts the pack into four piles and then mixes the cards by re-combining the piles. He or she then cuts the pack into two roughly equal sized packets that are shuffled together. This procedure is repeated. The spectator is then invited to deal out the cards into four piles. The outcome is that when the spectator examines the piles he or she finds that in each pile a Joker is the top card of the pile and an Ace is the bottom card.

Performance

1. Observe that as you now have the Aces you can get on with the tricks.
2. Take the pack, place it face-down on the table, and instruct the spectator to place the Aces face-down on top of the pack. Then instruct the spectator to cut off about the top ¾ of the pack and to place it to the right of the other cards (*from his or her point of view*). He or she should then cut off about ¾ of the cards of this second pile and place these to the right of the other two piles (*again from his or her point of view*). Finally, he or she should create a fourth pile by cutting off about the top half of the third pile. This pile he or she places to the right of the other 3 piles.

3. You now have (*from your point of view*):

   Pile A   Pile B   Pile C   Pile D
   (*NOTE: Pile D is the original bottom ¼ or so of the pack and Pile A is the original top ¼ or so of the pack.*)

4. There are now two ways of proceeding with the trick—the first involves the use of sleights-of-hand, the second does not. If you wish to use the first finish proceed directly to paragraphs 5 and 6 below; if you choose not to use sleights-of-hand proceed directly to paragraphs 7-11 below.

5. Place Pile A on Pile C and place Pile B on Pile D. Then place Pile AC on Pile BD. Then instruct the spectator to cut off about the top half of the face-down pack and to place it by the side of the bottom "half" of the pack. Take what was the top half of the pack in your left hand and the bottom half of the pack in your right hand and riffle shuffle them together. In performing the shuffle ensure that the bottom four cards of the right-hand packet fall first as a block and that the top four cards of the left-hand packet fall last as a block. (*For an explanation of this shuffle see the relevant sections in the chapter on "Handling and Sleights-of-Hand".*) Having performed the shuffle invite the spectator to cut the face-down pack again. You then repeat the shuffle described above. When the second shuffle has been completed hand the face-down pack to the spectator and instruct him or her to deal out four piles of face-down cards, dealing a card to each pile in turn.

6. Now ask the spectator what he or she would say if you forecast that the bottom card of each pile would be an Ace. Whatever the reply, say that you imagine it might be: "You must be joking!" Ask the spectator to turn over

the top card of each pile. (They will be Jokers.) Then ask the spectator to deal face-up each pile in turn. *(The bottom card will be an Ace.)*

7.   Instruct the spectator to turn Pile B face-up, and then to turn Pile C face-up. You then place Pile A on Pile C, then Pile B on Pile D, and then Pile AC on Pile BD. Having done this, instruct the spectator to cut off about the top half of the face-down pack and place it by the side of the bottom "half" of the pack. When he or she has done this, take the two packets and riffle shuffle them into each other. *(For an explanation of this shuffle see the relevant sections in the chapter on "Handling and Sleights-of-Hand".)*

8.   Now hand the pack to the spectator and get him or her to deal out the pack into two piles—one of the face-up cards and the other of face-down cards. When this has been done hand the face-down cards to the spectator and put the face-up cards aside. Now instruct the spectator to deal four piles of face-down cards, dealing a card to each pile in turn.

9.   When the deal is completed ask the spectator what he or she would have to say if you forecast that the bottom card of each pile would be an Ace. Irrespective of the response say that you imagine it would be "You must be joking!" *Instruct the spectator to turn over each pile. (The cards revealed will be Jokers.)* Then get the spectator to take each pile in turn and to deal out the cards from the top of the face-up pile. *(Each deal should finish with an Ace.)*

Third Trick:
"Card Sharper's Aces"

EFFECT

The Aces are placed face-down in the face-down pack which is then cut and re-assembled. In a series of deals the performer demonstrates how a card-sharper can manipulate the Aces. First he or she extracts three Aces from the pack and places them face-up on the table. He or she then places them in turn face-down between three other cards. When the packet is dealt out the Aces are the top three cards. The performer then places the three Aces face-down on top of the other three face-down cards and immediately deals the packet into two face-down piles, dealing a card to each pile in turn. When the first pile is examined the three Aces are revealed. Next, the pack is re-constituted and cut by the spectator. The performer then deals out five cards to himself and five cards to the spectator, dealing a card to each hand as determined by the spectator. When the hands are examined the performer has three Aces.

PERFORMANCE

1. Instruct the spectator to sort out the Aces and the Jokers and to put the Jokers in their appropriate carton. As he or she is doing this you collect the rest of the cards.
2. Now take the Aces from the spectator and place them on the table in a face-up pile with the two Black Aces

on the top of the pile. Then take each Ace in turn and place it face-down in the face-down pack, pushing each into the pack at the outer end, which you hold towards the spectators. In placing the cards into the pack the first two Aces (the Black Aces) should be placed in the bottom half of the pack and the last two Aces (the Red Aces) in the top half of the pack—the final Red Ace being placed in the pack as close to the top of the pack as possible, but not on the top. Now cut away the bottom ¼ of the face-down pack and place it on top of the pack. Then cut away the bottom half of the pack and place that packet on top of the pack. Finally, place the pack face-down on the table.

3. If you are not using a bridged card and sleights-of-hand in the performance of the routine proceed directly to paragraph 5 below.

4. If you are using a bridged card and sleights-of-hand there is an alternative method of handling to that set out at paragraph 2. If you wish to use it proceed as follows: collect the cards as described at paragraph 1 above and cut the bridged card to the bottom of the face-down pack and then place two face-down cards below it. Then instruct the spectator to place one of the Red Aces at the top, or bottom, or in the "middle" of the pack as described in the relevant section of the chapter on "Handling and Sleights-of-Hand". The spectator may then cut and complete the pack, at will. Finally, you cut the bridged card to the bottom of the pack, thus placing the Red Ace as the third card from the top in the face-down pack. Proceed now directly to paragraph 5 below.

5. Take some time in explaining that you are now going to demonstrate the way in which card-sharpers manipulate cards to their advantage. While you are

doing so pick up the pack from the table, turn it face-up and go through it, taking out the Aces as you come to them. Explain that to perform the demonstration you require only three Aces so extract only the first three Aces, which should be a Red Ace and two Black Aces. Hand these to the spectator as you come to them and instruct him or her to spread them out in a line face-up. While the spectator is doing this continue to spread the pack until you can see the second Red Ace, which should be very close to the bottom of the face-up pack. If there are only two cards below it close the pack, turn it face down, and place it on the table. If there are more than two cards below it slide the next two cards under the Ace, cut off the cards below those cards, and place them on top of the pack. Then turn the pack face-down and place it on the table. The second Red Ace should now be the third card from the top in the face down pack.

6. There are now three Aces face-up on the table. Pick them up and form them into a face-up pile with the Red Ace on top of the pile.

7. There are now two ways of performing the trick—one using the bridged card and sleights-of-hand, the other not using the bridged card and sleights-of-hand. If you are not using the bridged card and sleights-of-hand proceed directly to paragraph 9 below. If you choose to use the bridged card and sleights-of-hand proceed to paragraph 8 below.

8. In performing the trick you are going to use a handling technique known as a "double lift". (*A description of the handling required is set out in the relevant section of the chapter on "Handling and Sleights-of-Hand".*) Proceed as follows:

a. Pick up the face-down pack and take the top card, using the handling required for a double lift, **but using only the single top card**. Place this card face-down on the table. Let us assume it is 3S.

b. Now take what is the top card of the face-up pile of three Aces and hand this Ace (ie. the Red Ace) to the spectator. Instruct him or her to place it face-down on top of the face-down 3S.

c. Again, using the handling required for a double lift, **but using only a single card**, take the top card of the face-down pack and place this card face-down on top of the face-down Red Ace and the face-down 3S. Let us assume it is 5C.

d. Now take one of the face-up Black Aces and hand it to the spectator. Instruct him or her to place it face-down on top of the face-down 5C, Red Ace, and 3S. While he or she is doing this prepare a genuine double lift of what is now the top card of the face-down pack (ie. a Red Ace). Perform the double lift, revealing let us assume 2H. Place what the spectator assumes to be 2H (but is, in fact, a Red Ace) face-down on top of the face-down Black Ace, 5C, Red Ace, and 3S. Then instruct the spectator to place the final Black Ace face down on top of these face-down cards.

e. Point out to the spectator that you now have the three face-down Aces placed between the three other cards. Immediately, deal off face-down the top three cards of the face-down packet and instruct the spectator to turn them face-up. They will be three Aces—a Red Ace and two Black Aces.
    (NOTE: *The Red Ace is, of course, a different Red Ace to the one the spectator placed face-down on the cards but it is surprising how few spectators*

will notice this. In any case, even if they do, they will still be mystified as to how that Ace has suddenly appeared. However, you may, if you wish, hide the identity of the second Red Ace. To do this instead of allowing the spectator to turn over the face-down cards pick them up yourself. The Red Ace will be the middle card of the packet and by over-lapping the cards along their length it is possible to display them with only the "A"s of the Red Ace index being visible.)

f.   Immediately turn the three Aces face-down and place them on top of the three cards you have not dealt out. Point out that this places the three Aces as the top three cards of the packet. Then deal out the cards of the packet face-down onto the table into two three-card hands, dealing a card to each hand in turn, observing, as you do so, that this will distribute the Aces between the hands. When the deal is finished instruct the spectator to turn the hand to which you dealt first face-up. It will contain three Aces—a Red Ace and two Black Aces.

(Note: This time the Red Ace will be the Red Ace the spectator originally placed on the cards.)

g.   To conclude the trick place the three cards that have not been turned face-up face-down on the face-down pack. *(Note: From the handling at paragraph 4 above the bridged card is the bottom card of the pack.)* You now allow the spectator to place each of the three Aces individually back into the pack either on the top, or the bottom, or in the "middle". As each Ace is placed in the pack the spectator may cut and complete the pack at will—and in each case you cut the pack to take the bridged card to the bottom of the pack. *(For the handling required see the relevant section of the chapter "Handling and Sleights-of-Hand".*)

h. You now tell the spectator that you are going to play a hand of Blind Poker. Explain that what you are going to do is to deal one card to begin: do so, dealing the top card of the pack face-down to the spectator and the second card to yourself. You then explain that you will deal either one or two cards next as the spectator chooses: demonstrate this by first of all dealing off face-down a single card to the spectator and then a single card to yourself, and then dealing off two cards to the spectator and two cards to yourself. This will mean that you then need one card each to make up the Poker hand of five cards: deal off the next card to the spectator and then the next card to yourself. Immediately pick up the spectator's hand, place it on top of yours and place the combined packet on top of the face-down pack. Then perform a Charlier Shuffle. (*For a description of this shuffle see the relevant section of the chapter "Handling and Sleights-of-Hand".*) After allowing the spectator to cut and complete the pack you cut the bridged card to the bottom of the pack. (*For an explanation of the term "cut and complete" see the "Introduction".*)

i. Now deal the top card of the pack face-down to the spectator and the next card face-down to yourself. Then remind the spectator that he or she may choose to receive either one or two cards. Deal face down to the spectator the number of cards chosen and the same number to yourself. Continue dealing in this way until you both have five cards.

j. Instruct the spectator to turn his or her cards over. He or she may or may not have a good hand, but it is unlikely to be better than yours, which will have three Aces.

9. To perform the trick not using a bridged card and sleights-of-hand proceed as follows:

   a. Pick up the face-down pack, take the top card and place it face-down on the table. In doing so, "inadvertently" allow the spectator to glimpse the face of the card.

   b. Instruct the spectator to place the Red Ace face-down on top of the card you have just placed on the table. Now take the next card at the top of the pack and place it face-down on top of the two face-down cards on the table, again "inadvertently" allowing the spectator to glimpse the face of the card.

   c. Instruct the spectator to place a Black Ace face-down on top of the face-down cards on the table. You then take what is now the top card of the face-down pack (**this time without allowing the spectator to see the face of the card**) and place it face-down on top of the pile of cards on the table. The spectator then adds the second Black Ace face-down to the top of the pile. (*Note: To distract the spectator's attention as you place the top card of the pack on the pile you may, if you wish, at the same time pass the pack to the spectator and ask him or her to shuffle it and place it aside.*)

   d. You now continue the trick as described at paragraph 8e and 8f above.

   e. To conclude the trick place the three cards that have not been turned face-up face-down onto the face-down pack. In doing so, take the opportunity to note the identity of the bottom card of the pack.

Then take the three face-up Aces and place these cards face-down on top of the pack. Having done this perform a Charlier Shuffle. (*For a description of how to do this see the relevant section of the chapter "Handling and Sleights-of-Hand".*) The spectator may now cut-and-complete the pack, at will. (*For an explanation of the term "cut and complete" see the "Introduction".*) When he or she has done so, take the pack, turn it face-up and spread it to show the mix of the cards. In making this spread do not push the cards along the top of the face-up pack—pull the cards along the bottom of the pack using the fingers beneath the pack. Continue with the spread until you see the card you noted the identity of above.

f. Split the pack at that point and take that card and all the cards below it to what will be the bottom of the face-down pack.

g. Conclude the trick as described at paragraph 8h, 8i, and 8j above, using the card you identified at paragraph 9e above (which will still be at the bottom of the pack) as a key card. (*For an explanation of how the key card is used see the relevant section in the chapter on "Handling and Sleights-of-Hand".*)

Fourth Trick: "Telepathic Aces"

EFFECT

A spectator is invited to extract the two Red Aces from a pack. He or she then shuffles the pack and inserts one of the Red Aces face-up anywhere in the pack and then shuffles the pack again. He or she then places the second Red Ace face-up in the pack next to the card either below or above the other Ace. The pack is then replaced in its carton. The performer now takes another pack and extracts the two Red Aces which the spectator then replaces face-up in the pack. He or she then cuts the pack at will. The spectator is now asked to take the first pack out of its carton and identify the card between the two face-up Aces. He or she is then asked to identify the card between the two face-up Aces in the second pack. The two cards will be identical.

PERFORMANCE

1. For this trick you require the two packs of full-sized cards and, if you have one, a Miniature-sized pack, and some rubber bands. However, the trick can be performed with only the two full-sized packs. (*NOTE: The success of the trick depends upon the cards being in good condition.*)

2. Take the pack you have been using for the previous tricks, re-constitute it, and place it face-down on the table. Take the other full-sized pack out of its carton, extract the Joker cards, shuffle it thoroughly, and

place it face-down on the table by the side of the other pack.

3. If you are using a Miniature pack take that pack from its carton, extract any Joker cards and any other extraneous cards from it, shuffle it thoroughly, and place it face-down on the table.

4. If you are using a Miniature pack invite the spectator to take that pack, shuffle it, and then to extract from it the two Red Aces. He or she should then shuffle the pack again and insert one of the Red Aces *face-up* anywhere into the face-down pack, leaving it protruding for about half its length. He or she should then insert the other Red Ace (*again face-up*) next to the card either below or above the other Red Ace. The second Red Ace should also protrude from the pack for about half its length. Now, if you have one, place a rubber band around the pack. (*NOTE: You now have a card in the Miniature pack sandwiched between two Red Aces.*) Take the pack in your right hand with the face of the cards towards you and the faces of the reversed Aces towards the spectator, carefully covering the base of the pack and the area below it with the back of the hand. Your thumb should be across the face of the card facing you, about ¾ of the way down the pack. Your first finger should be at the bottom inner corner with the other three fingers below the level of the bottom end of the pack. If you wish, you may place the index and second finger of the left hand over the index and second finger of the right hand with the other two fingers of the left hand below the level of the little finger of the right hand.

5. You now instruct the spectator to push the two Aces together into the pack. (*This action will "pump-push" the card between the two Aces out at the bottom of the pack.*) Note the identity of this card (*which is covered*

from the view of the spectators by the back of the right hand) and, while the spectator is handing you the Miniature pack carton, push this card back into the pack.

6. You then hand the pack to the spectator, who places it into its carton, which is then placed aside.

7. If you are not using a Miniature pack go through exactly the same procedure as described in paragraphs 4, 5, and 6 above with one of the full-sized packs.

8. Now take one of the full-sized packs (or, if you are not using a Miniature pack, the remaining full-sized pack), turn it face up and go through it to extract the two Red Aces. In fact, what you are also doing is locating the card you noted at paragraph 5 above. When you do locate the card, you should cut the pack to place this card as the bottom card of the face-down pack.

9. The spectator now places one of the Red Aces face-up either on the top or at the bottom of the pack as he or she wishes, and then cuts and completes the pack, at will. (*For an explanation of the term "cut and complete" see the "Introduction".*) Finally, you instruct the spectator to go through the face-down pack, locate the face-up Ace, and to then place the second Red Ace face-up on top of the first face-down card above the first Red Ace. You then take the pack and, if you have one, place a rubber band around it before placing it in its appropriate carton.

10. If you are not using a Miniature pack proceed directly to paragraph 12 below. If you are using a Miniature pack now take the remaining full-sized pack and repeat the procedure described in paragraph 8 above. Then take one of the Red Aces and place it face-up on top of the face-down pack, the Ace projecting forward from the pack by about half its length. You then cut

and complete the pack to take the projecting Ace to about the centre of the pack. Now spread the face-down pack to allow the spectator to place the other Red Ace (face-up) on top of the first face-down card above the first red Ace. If you have one, now place a rubber band around the pack. In any case, return the pack to its appropriate carton with the two Red Aces projecting from the carton end. (*For a definition of "cut and complete" see the "Introduction".*)

11. As you have been using a Miniature pack you should proceed as follows:

   a. Instruct the spectator to take the Miniature pack out of its carton, to remove the rubber band (if used), and to identify the card between the two Aces.

   b. Next instruct the spectator take the first full-sized pack used out of its carton, to remove the rubber band (if used), and to identify the card between the two Aces.

   c. The spectator should then take the second full-sized pack used and push the projecting Aces into the carton. He or she then removes the pack from the carton, removes the rubber band (if used), and identifies the card between the two Aces.

   d. The cards between the two Aces should be identical.

12. As you have not been using a Miniature pack you should proceed as follows:

   a. Instruct the spectator to take the first full-sized pack used out of its carton, to remove the rubber band (if used) and to identify the card between the two Aces.

b. The spectator should then repeat this process with the second full-sized pack.

c. The cards between the two Aces should be identical.

Fifth Trick:
"Just Think of An Ace"

Effect

The spectator extracts the four Aces from the pack and they are placed face-up on the table. The remainder of the pack is shuffled and the Aces, in turn, are returned face-down to the pack, which is cut by the spectator after each Ace has been replaced. Four piles of cards are then dealt out face-down from the pack and the spectator is invited to reconstitute the pack by determining the way in which the piles are combined. The spectator is then invited to think of any of the Aces which is then spelled out using the top cards of the pack.

Performance

1. The reader will note that this trick is used as one of the "four-trick any-pack" tricks in the routine described in the chapter *"Old Wine In A New Bottle"*. However, as it features a particularly strong revelation of an Ace it also fits well into this routine with some very minor differences in the handling and presentation.

2. To begin allow the spectator to choose any of the two full-sized packs and to extract the four Aces from it. You then take the Aces and place them face-up on the table in a fan formation with the AC at the bottom of the fan, the AH on top of it, the AS next, and the AD as the top card of the face-up fan. (Note: *Useful mnemonics*

that could help you to remember the order are: **C** – **H** – *a* – **S** – *e* – **D** *or the phrase "**C**urly **H**air **S**ettles **D**own".*)

3. Pick up the remainder of the pack and shuffle it. Then allow the spectator to shuffle it.

4. If you are performing the routine not using sleights-of-hand and a bridged card proceed directly to paragraph 10. If you are using sleights-of-hand and a bridged card proceed directly to the next paragraph.

5. Instruct the spectator to think of any one of the Aces. Collect the Aces together and turn them face-down. (*They are now from the top AC, AH, AS, and AD.*)

6. Take each Ace separately off the pile and place it in the "middle" of the pack under the control of the bridged card, which each time you cut to the bottom of the pack. (*For an explanation of how to use the bridged card in this way see the relevant sections in the chapter on "Handling and Sleights-of-Hand".*) On the final cut of the bridged card to the bottom of the pack the cards at the top of the face-down pack are in the order AD, AS, AH, and AC. The spectator may now cut and complete the pack at will—provided that, finally, you cut the bridged card to the bottom of the pack. (*For an explanation of the term "cut and complete" see the "Introduction".*)

7. Now deal of the top 13 cards of the face-down pack into a face-down pile (Pile A), then the next 13 cards into a second face-down pile (Pile B), then the next 13 cards into a third face-down pile (Pile C), and then place the next and final 13 cards on the table *without dealing them out* (Pile D). (*NOTE: The Aces are now at the bottom of Pile A and the bridged card is at the bottom of Pile D.*)

8. Your aim now is to produce a face-down pack with Pile A at the top of the pack. This can be achieved as follows:

  a. Allow the spectator a free choice of any two piles which are then combined—as are the other two piles. However, in the case of Pile A and Pile D, the Pile D goes on top of Pile A; in other combinations Pile A goes on top and Pile D on the bottom.

  b. The spectator may then place any combined pair on the top or bottom of any other combined pair. He or she may then cut and complete the pack, at will.

  c. If you then cut the bridged card to the bottom of the pack Pile A will be at the top of the pack.

9. The pack is now configured to allow the spectator's thought-of-Ace to be spelled out as follows:

  a. "A-C-E-O-F-C-L-U-B-S"
     Take a card off the top of the pack for each letter. AC is the card at the "S" of the spelling.

  b. "A-C-E-O-F-H-E-A-R-T-S"
     The AH is at the "S" of the spelling.

  c. "A-C-E-O-F-S-P-A-D-E-S"
     AS is the *next card in the pack*, ie. the top card of the pack after the spelling out of the card.

  d. "A-C-E-O-F-D-I-A-M-O-N-D-S"
     AD is at the "S" of the spelling.

10. As you are not using sleights-of-hand and a bridged card to perform the routine you will need to employ a subterfuge to control the cards. This is provided for in the handling set out in the following paragraphs.

11. The position is that there are four face-up Aces in a fan on the table and you have the remaining 48 cards of the pack. Deal out these 48 cards into four face-down piles of 12 cards each and invite the spectator to turn the face-up fan of Aces face-down and place it on top of any one of the piles. Instruct him or her to then think of and remember any one of the Aces. Then he or she should place any one of the other three piles on top of the pile on which he or she has placed the Aces. The other two piles are put aside.

12. You now take the combined pile of face-down cards containing the Aces and mix it as follows:

     a. From the top of the pack deal four cards face-down in a pile on the table. Then from the bottom deal off face-down onto the pile of four cards. Continue this process of dealing alternately from the top and then the bottom of the block of cards until you have only four cards left—deal these onto the top of the face-down pile.

     b. Pick up the pile and as you do so note the bottom card of the packet. Now perform a Charlier Shuffle. (*For a description of how this is done see the relevant section of the chapter "Handling and Sleights-of-Hand".*) When the shuffle has been completed turn the packet face-up and spread it to show the mix of the cards. In performing this spread move the cards from the bottom of the packet from right to left, each card sliding above the preceding card. Continue with the spread until you locate the card you noted above. Cut the spread at that point so as to place the noted card at the bottom card of the face-down pack.

13. Immediately deal off face-down onto the table the top 13 cards of the packet. Keep what is left of the packet in your hand. Now ask the spectator: "Which of the packets do you want?" If the spectator chooses the pile you have dealt out onto the table discard the cards you have in your hand. If he or she chooses the cards you have in your hand give them to him or her and immediately pick up the pile on the table.

14. Having picked up the pile from the table ask the spectator to name his or her thought-of Ace. You proceed to spell out the Ace using the spelling system set out at paragraph 9 above. As you spell out the thought-of Ace you should place the cards as they are being removed to the bottom of the packet.

Sixth Trick:
"All Together Now"

EFFECT

The eight Aces are extracted from two packs. A half of one pack is taken and shuffled into the half of the other pack. The cards are then placed face-up on the table and the spectator inserts the Aces face-down in turn into the face-up packet which is then cut into two roughly equal packets. A series of shuffles follows with cards being turned face-up and face-down in an arbitrary way. After the final shuffle the spectator extracts the face-down cards. They are the eight Aces.

PERFORMANCE

1. This trick is performed using the two full-sized packs. Re-constitute them, extract the Aces and then shuffle them. Then place the two packs side by side.

2. Invite the spectator to cut off about half of each pack and to place these cards aside. You take the cards that are left and riffle shuffle them into each other. Having done so you place the combined packet **face-up** on the table. (*For an explanation of the term "riffle shuffle" see the relevant sections in the chapter on "Handling and Sleights-of-Hand".*)

3. The spectator is now asked to turn the Aces **face-down** and to insert them individually into the packet. You then take the packet, cut it roughly in half, and riffle shuffle one half into the other half. You then cut the shuffled

packet roughly in half and place the top half (Pile A) to your left and the bottom half (Pile B) to your right. In placing Pile B on the table turn it over without drawing attention to this move.

4. Now cut off about half of the cards from the top of Pile A and place them by the side of Pile B. In doing so, make it quite clear that you are turning them over. Do the same with Pile B, placing the cards by the side of Pile A.

5. Invite the spectator to shuffle the cards by the side of Pile A into that pile, while you riffle shuffle the cards by the side of Pile B into that pile.

6. Now repeat paragraphs 4 and 5 at least one more time. After the final repetition, in placing Pile B on the table turn it over—again without drawing attention to this move.

7. Now take the two piles and riffle shuffle them into each other. (*Note: The eight Aces should now be face-down in the packet of otherwise face-up cards.*)

8. Hand the packet (face-up) to the spectator, instructing him or her to go through it and to extract any face-down cards, placing each face-down card face-down in a pile on the table according to the colour of its back. He or she should end the sorting out of the packet with a pile of four cards of one colour back and four cards of the other colour back. When the piles are turned face-up each will contain the four Aces of the relevant pack.

Adaptations And Alternatives

The context in which card magic is performed largely determines the tricks that can be used and the effects that can be achieved. The performer who plies his trade in the theatre is likely to use a larger-than-life style of presentation with tricks that appeal more by the strength of their outcomes rather than any direct involvement of the audience. He or she may also be able to achieve effects by manipulations and sleights-of-hand that would be fool-hardy if performed in close proximity to the spectators. However, most performers present their tricks to a small number of people—usually in a social group seated around a table. In these circumstances the performer should attempt with each trick to involve all the spectators. In this way not only is their interest in the performance enhanced but their direct involvement distracts their attention from the mechanics of the trick. In other words they are more concerned with what is being done rather than how it is being done. In addition, in such a setting attempts to deceive the spectators by intricate handling or by complex sleights-of-hand are unlikely to be successful. Ideally, what is required are self-working tricks with a minimum of manipulation.

The tricks described in the preceding sections of this chapter meet most of these criteria for performance before a small audience. The one requirement they do not meet is the total involvement of the audience if that audience is more than one spectator. However, the tricks are easily adapted to involve additional spectators. For example, in the first trick, "*Finding The Aces*", three spectators could be involved—one for each of the Aces to be found from the pack. A fourth spectator could be involved if the three spectators handed their cards face-down to that spectator to whom you also handed the fourth and final Ace. Alternatively, the first three spectators could retain their face-down cards and, after you have handed the final face-down card to the fourth spectator, they could all turn their cards face-up to reveal the Aces. Similarly, in the second, fourth, and sixth tricks (*"You Must Be Joking"*, *"Telepathic Aces"*, *and "All Together Now"*) there are a number of occasions in the course of the presentation when a second, third, or even fourth spectator could be invited to perform whatever procedure is required at that point.

The third trick, *"Chard Sharper's Aces"*, is very much a presentation by the performer—although even with this trick it would be possible to involve three spectators, each placing an Ace in turn onto the pile before the deal is made. However, if this was done, it would be necessary to ensure that the cards were distributed to the spectators in such a way that the Aces were placed in the appropriate order.

The fifth trick, *"Just Think of An Ace"*, could be adapted to involve up to four spectators, but great care would need to be taken to prevent such an adaptation revealing how the effect was being achieved. Probably the safest way of adapting the trick is to proceed as follows:

a. Invite each of up to four spectators to think of an Ace.

b. Allow different spectators to choose how the piles are combined.

c. In spelling out the thought-of Aces, take the cards off the top of the packet without disturbing their order and, after the Ace has been revealed, place it back face-down on top of the pack. Then place all the other cards face-down on top of the face-down pack.

d. Use a bridged card or a key card to allow the packet to be cut and completed after the return of the cards to the pack. *(For an explanation of how to use a bridged card or a key card see the relevant sections in the chapter on "Handling and Sleights-of-Hand".)*

For those readers who do not wish to adapt the tricks in this way alternative or additional tricks are described below—each designed to involve a specific number of spectators:

a. *"Magic Clocks"* - two spectators.
b. *"Spell Them Out"* - three spectators.
c. *"More Aces"* - four spectators.
d. *"Everybody's Ace"* - any number of spectators

"Magic Clocks"
(For Two Spectators)

Effect

The first spectator shuffles a Blue-backed pack, the second spectator shuffles a Red-backed pack. Using the appropriate pack for each spectator the performer spreads the cards face-up to show the mix of the cards and then invites the spectator to cut off from the top of the face-down pack as many cards as he or she wishes and to retain them. From what is left of each pack the performer deals off onto the table 12 cards face-down in the form of the face of a clock. Each spectator now counts the cards they cut off and takes the card of the appropriate clock face that corresponds to this number. When these cards are turned over they are identical Aces.

Performance

1.   For this trick you require two packs of cards—say one Blue-backed and the other Red-backed. Take the Blue-backed pack, hand it to the first spectator and invite him or her to give it a thorough shuffle. Do the same using the Red-backed pack with the second spectator.

2.   Take the Blue-backed pack from the first spectator and turn it face-up. You now spread out the pack to show the mix of the cards. You perform this spread with both hands (palms up) beneath the pack with the thumbs on the face of the cards. The spread is made by moving the cards from right to left (*from your point of view*)

using the right thumb, ie. the cards are spread moving each card underneath the preceding card. When you come to an Ace (preferably about the middle of the pack) draw this Ace under the left-hand cards using the fingers of the left hand. Continue to spread the cards using the right thumb but exert sufficient pressure on the left-hand of the spread to prevent any further cards being forced underneath the selected Ace. When the spread is completed separate the pack at the point at which the selected Ace is the bottom card of the left-hand spread. Split the pack at this point, moving the right-hand packet to the right, and then place this packet on top of the left-hand packet. Now turn the pack face-down and place it on the table. (*NOTE: If the procedure described above has been correctly performed the selected Ace is now the top card of the face-down pack.*)

3. Repeat the procedure using the Red-backed pack, placing the identical Ace to the top of the face-down pack. If on the initial spread of the face-up cards the identical Ace is not conveniently positioned cut the pack to place it at a convenient point and spread the cards again.

4. Now deal from the top of the face-down packs the top 12 cards of the Blue-backed pack in front of the first spectator and the top 12 cards of the Red-backed pack in front of the second spectator. As you do so explain to them that you want each of them to cut off a packet of cards from the top of their face-down piles. Also explain to them that neither you nor they should know how many cards they have cut off. Suggest that they should immediately put them into a pocket or sit on them.

5. When this has been done place the remaining cards of each pile (**without disturbing their order**) face-down

on top of the appropriate face-down pack. As you pick up each pack to replace the cards secretly note the identity of the bottom card of each pack.

6. Each pack is then placed face-down on the table and the spectators are invited to cut and complete their packs, at will. (*For an explanation of the term "cut and complete" see the "Introduction".*) When this has been done take each pack, turn it face-up, and spread it to show the mix of the cards. In doing so, locate the card in each pack that you noted at paragraph 5 above and cut the pack to place this card at the bottom card of the face-down pack.

7. For each face-down pack now deal out the top 12 cards onto the table in the form of a clock. In placing the cards you should begin at the 11 o'clock position and then place the cards anti-clockwise, ie., 10 o'clock, 9 o'clock, 8 o'clock etc. The 12th and final card for each pack is placed in the 12 o'clock position.

8. Invite each spectator to take the cards he or she cut off at paragraph 4 above and to count them. When they have done this instruct them to take the card in the appropriate clock at the hour corresponding to the number of cards they cut off. They should place the two cards face-down side by side.

9. Now instruct them to turn the cards face-up. When they do so they will find that they have arrived at identical Aces.

"Spell Them Out"
(For Three Spectators)

EFFECT

Using two packs, each of which is thoroughly shuffled, the performer invites the spectators to choose one of the packs (say, the Red-backed pack) and to extract from it the Aces. The performer then takes the Ace of Diamonds and places it face-up in front of him- or herself. The other three Aces are mixed together face-down and one is placed face-down in front of each of the three spectators. The performer then takes the other pack (say, the Blue-backed pack), passes it to the spectators and instructs them to deal out onto the table four piles of face-down cards. The pack is then re-constituted by the spectators placing the piles one on the other in any order they wish. A spectator now places his or her face-down Ace on top of the face-down Blue-backed pack and the pack is shuffled and then cut to place the Red-backed Ace as the top card of the pack. The Red-backed Ace is turned over to reveal its identity and this identity is spelled out by removing cards from the top of the pack. The card arrived at is placed face-down on the table and the procedure is repeated for the other two spectators. This having been done, the "Ace of Diamonds" is spelled out from the pack. A further card is removed from the pack. To conclude the trick the performer deals out and reveals all the cards that have been removed from the pack. They are the eight Aces.

PERFORMANCE

1. For this trick you require two packs of cards—say, one Blue-backed and the other Red-backed. Both packs are separately and thoroughly shuffled. The spectators then select one of the packs. You split this pack roughly into three equal packets and hand a packet to each of the three spectators, instructing them to extract the Aces and to place the remaining cards aside. While they are doing this you "play" with the other pack and, as you are doing so, you place the Aces of that pack face-down on top of the pack. The order in which the Aces are placed is immaterial.

2. Take the Aces the spectators have separated out from their pack, say the Red-backed pack. Extract AD and place it face-up in front of yourself. Then take the other three Aces, turn them face-down, mix them, and allow each spectator to choose a card, which they should place face-down in front of themselves. The remaining Red-backed cards are placed aside.

3. Now place the Blue-backed pack face-down in front of the first spectator and instruct him or her to cut off about the top $1/_3$ of the pack and to deal the cards he or she has cut off into four piles, dealing a card to each pile in turn. Instruct the second spectator to cut off about half of what is left of the pack and do the same, continuing to deal them from the point at which the first spectator finished his or her deal. The third spectator is then invited to take the remaining cards of the Red-backed pack and to continue the deal from the point at which the second spectator finished his or her deal. When the dealing has been completed, consolidate the pack by picking up the piles in any order as determined by the spectators.

4. Having done so you instruct the first spectator to place his or her card face-down on top of the pack and to cut and complete the pack. You then perform a Charlier Shuffle, after which you invite the spectator to cut and complete the pack again. Once he or she has done so, go through the pack to locate the Red-backed card and cut the pack to place this card as the top card of the face-down pack. Then turn it face-up to reveal its identity. (*For an explanation of the term "cut and complete" see the "Introduction" and for a description of the Charlier Shuffle see the chapter "Handling and Sleights-of-Hand".*)

5. You now proceed to spell out the identity of the Ace, using the following system of spelling:

   a. "T-H-E-A-C-E-O-F H-E-A-R-T-S", "T-H-E-A-C-E-O-F S-P-A-D-E-S", etc., as appropriate, taking the face-up card as the first letter of the spelling, moving each card to the hand not holding the pack, and placing each card under the preceding card.

   b. If you are spelling out AH or AS when you come to the "S" of the spelling leave that card face-down on the pack, place the pack on the table, turn the face-up card of the counted-out packet face-down and place it in front of yourself. Then place the Blue-backed cards of the packet aside. Now pick up the pack, take the top card, and place it face-down somewhere in the middle of the table.

   c. If you are spelling out AC, when you come to the "S" of the spelling you take *all* the cards of the spelling into the hand not holding the pack before placing the pack on the table. You then proceed as in paragraph 5b above.

6. You now repeat the whole procedure as described in paragraphs 4 and 5 above for the second and then the third spectator.

7. The situation you have now arrived at is that there are three face-down Blue-backed cards in the middle of the table and the remaining cards of the Blue-backed pack face-down on the table. In front of you are three face-down Red-backed cards and a face-up Red-backed AD.

8. Point out that only AD remains. Pick it up and place it face-down on top of the other three Red-backed cards. Then place all four Red-backed cards on top of the remaining cards of the Blue-backed pack. Pick up this packet and turn the top card face-up (ie. AD) and proceed to spell out "T-H-E-A-C-E-O-F D-I-A-M-O-N-D-S" using the spelling procedure described at paragraph 5a. above. However, in this case do not transfer the cards from the pack to the hand not holding the pack. Instead transfer each card as it is spelled out to the bottom of the packet of cards. When the spelling is completed there will be a face-down Blue-backed card at the top of the packet.

9. Take this card from the top of the packet and place it face-down with the other three face-down cards in the middle of the table. Underneath it will be a face-up AD, turn it face-down and place it with the four face-down Blue-backed cards in the middle of the table. The next three cards in the packet will be the three Red-backed cards, place these three cards with the other face-down cards in the middle of the table and place the remaining Blue-backed cards of the packet aside.

10. Now pick up all the face-down cards in the middle of the table and deal them out into a face-up pile. You will deal out eight Aces.

"More Aces"
(For Four Spectators)

EFFECT

The pack is mixed and spread face-up to show the mix of the cards. It is then cut into four roughly equal packets and a packet is placed in front of each of the four spectators. The packets are then mixed by each spectator dealing cards from his or her own packet onto the other packets. This having been done, the four spectators, each using a different arbitrary procedure, arrive at a card in their packet. When the cards are revealed they are the four Aces.

PERFORMANCE

1. Ideally this trick follows one in which two packs have been used. This will allow you to invite the spectator to reconstitute one of the packs and return it to its carton while you reconstitute the other pack. As you are doing so you should secretly place the four Aces face-down on top of the face-down pack (and, if you are using it, the bridged card at the bottom of the pack).

2. If you are not using a bridged card proceed directly to paragraph 4. If you are using a bridged card proceed directly to the next paragraph. (*For an explanation of the term "bridged card" see the "Introduction" and the chapter on "Handling and Sleights-of-Hand".*)

3. False mix the pack using the handling described in the relevant section of the chapter "*Handling and Sleights-of-Hand*".

4. Turn the pack face up and spread it out to show the mix of the pack. As you do this take care not to display the Aces which will be the bottom four cards of the face-up pack.

5. Place the pack face-down on the table and invite a spectator to cut it into four roughly equal face-down piles in the following manner: he or she first of all cuts off about the top ¾ of the pack, leaving Pile A (what was the bottom of the pack), they then cut off about ¾ of the rest of the pack, leaving Pile B, then the top half of the remainder of the pack, leaving Pile C. The packet that remains (what was the top of the pack) is Pile D.

6. Pile A is placed in front of the first spectator, Pile B in front of the second spectator, Pile C in front of the third spectator, and Pile D in front of the fourth spectator.

7. The first spectator now takes Pile A and deals a card from it face-down in front of the other three piles and then places his or her remaining cards face-down in front of him- or herself. Each of the three piles is then placed face-down on top of the card in front of it. The first spectator then takes Pile A again and deals a card from the top of it face-down onto the top of the three piles. He or she then places the remaining cards face-down in front of him- or herself.

8. The second spectator now takes Pile B and repeats the procedure described in paragraph 7 above. The third spectator does the same with Pile C, and, finally, the fourth spectator does the same with Pile D.
   (NOTE: *The Aces are now the top cards of each of the piles and the trick could be brought to a satisfactory conclusion at this point. However, a much stronger finish can be produced by continuing as described below.*)

9. Instruct the first spectator to cut off from the top of his or her face-down pile about half the cards and to place

them face-down by the side of the remaining cards. You take the remaining cards, turn them face-up, and place them across the face-down cards to form a cross.

10. Now turn to the second spectator. Pick up his or her face-down cards and count the number of cards in the packet without reversing their order (*see the "Introduction" for an explanation of how this is done*). You then invite the spectator to think of and state any number below this total number of cards. When he or she has done so, count the number of cards corresponding to the stated number off the top of the face-down packet **without reversing their order**. Place the cards you have counted off face-down on the table, turn the remaining cards face-up, and place them across the face-down cards to form a cross.

11. Turn now to the third spectator. Instruct him or her to cut off as many cards as he or she wishes from their face-down pile and to turn them face-up. You then take the face-down cards and place them on top of the face-up cards—then turn the packet over. The spectator again cuts off as many cards as he or she wishes from the top of the packet and turns them over. You place the remaining cards of the packet on top of them—and then turn the whole packet over. You then instruct the spectator to take the first face-up card from the top of the packet and to place it across the top of the packet to form a cross.

12. Finally, invite the fourth spectator to deal off face-down onto the table as many cards as he or she wishes from the top of his or her packet. When this has been done place the undealt cards aside. Then instruct the spectator to deal the cards he or she has counted out into two face-down piles. Note the pile to which the last card is dealt: this pile will have the Ace as its top card.

Now invite the spectator to place one of the piles on top of the cards you put aside. If the spectator places the pile with the Ace on top of the other cards then instruct him or her to place all these cards on top of the pile he or she has retained. If the spectator places the pile without the Ace on top of the other cards then instruct him or her to place the pile he or she has retained on top of the other cards. In either case, the pile with the Ace becomes the top cards of the combined packet. The spectator is now invited to take the top card of the packet and to place it across the top of the packet to form a cross.

13. You now have the fourth spectator's packet with a single face-down card across the top of it and the other three spectators' packets with face-up cards across the top of face-down cards.

14. Instruct the first, second, and third spectators to remove the face-up cards from their piles and to turn over the first face-down card. They will all be Aces.

15. Finally, instruct the fourth spectator to turn over the face down card on top of his or her packet. It will be the fourth Ace.

"Everybody's Ace"
(For Any Number of Spectators)

EFFECT

The pack is thoroughly shuffled and spread face-up to show the mix of the cards. Any number of spectators then, in turn, each using a different arbitrary procedure, arrives at a card which they secretly note and return to the pack. When all have noted a card the pack is given to each in turn and each of them is invited to cut the pack. The performer then takes the pack and deals out face-down onto the table the same number of cards as there are spectators. This packet is passed to each spectator who examines the cards and confirms that his or her card is one of the cards in the packet. The performer then deals out the cards face-up onto the table and invites the spectators all together to shout out and pick up their card. They all shout out and attempt to pick up the same Ace.

PERFORMANCE

1. Each spectator involved is handed the pack of cards and instructed to shuffle it.
2. You take back the pack from the last spectator involved, shuffle it, and spread it face-up to show the mix of the cards. In doing so, note the position of a conveniently placed Ace and cut the cards at the point that places this Ace as the top card of the face-down pack.
3. Place the pack face-down on the table and instruct the first spectator to take the top card. Instruct him or her

to note it secretly without revealing it to either you or to any of the other spectators. When he or she has done so instruct him or her to place the card face-down on top of the face-down pack.

4. A second spectator is instructed to cut off about half of the pack, which he or she should place face-down on the table. Now instruct the spectator to take the bottom part of the packet, to turn it face-up, and to place it on top of the packet he or she has just cut off. Finally, you instruct him or her to turn over the whole packet. You then take the pack and cut it exactly in the same way, including the final turning over of the whole packet. (NOTE: *When you make your cut you should ensure that you are cutting below the level at which the spectator cut.*) When you have completed the whole procedure you place the pack in front of the spectator and instruct him or her to take the first face-down card in the pack. He or she should note the card secretly without revealing it to either you or to any of the other spectators. When the spectator has done this, instruct him or her to place the card face-down on the table, to turn any face-up cards in the pack face-down, and **to place the face-down pack on top of it**.

5. You now take the face-down pack, cut off about the top ¾ of the cards, turn these cards over, and place them at the bottom of the pack. You then turn the pack over, cut off about the top ½ of the cards, turn these cards over and place them at the bottom of the pack. You then turn the whole pack over and spread it until you locate the first face-up card. You cut the pack at this point leaving the face-down card above the face-up card in place. The other face-down cards above that card you turn over and place at the bottom of the pack. You then place the pack on the table and instruct the third

spectator to take the top card of the pack and to note it secretly without revealing it to either you or the other spectators. When the spectator has done this instruct him or her to place the card on top of the pack. Then go through the pack and turn any face-up cards face-down. Having done this, place the pack face-down on the table.

6. Immediately turn to the fourth spectator and, as you do, pick up the pack and begin dealing cards from the top of the pack face-down in a pile on the table, counting them mentally as you do. Once you have passed 10 instruct the spectator to stop you dealing at whatever point he or she wishes. When he or she has done so, stop the deal at that point, and instruct him or her to cut off from the top of the pile as many cards as he or she wishes and immediately either put them in a pocket or hide them away. Point out that this is because you do not want to know how many cards have been taken nor do you want him or her to know. When this has been done begin dealing out cards again onto the pile and again ask the spectator to stop the deal at any point. When he or she has done so ask him or her again to cut off any number of cards from the top of the pile and again to hide them away. Now take the cards remaining on the pile and place them on top of the remaining cards of the pack—as you do this (or at some convenient time before) note the identity of the bottom card of the pack. Now perform a Charlier Shuffle of the face-down pack. Then turn the pack face-up and perform a second Charlier Shuffle. As you do, spread the blocks of cards as you take them from the pack so that you are able to locate the card you identified above. When you do so place that block (with the identified card as its face card) as the top block of the face-up pack, which will result in

that card being the bottom card of the face-down pack. *(For an explanation of how to perform a Charlier Shuffle see the relevant section of the chapter on "Handling and Sleights-of-Hand".)* Now immediately deal out into a face-down pile on the table a number of cards equal to the cards previously dealt out in the first and second deal. You do this without counting out aloud or stating the number. You then instruct the spectator to take the cards he or she has cut off and hidden and to count them. While the spectator is counting his or her cards pick up the pile you have dealt onto the table and place it on top of the pack. You then count off from the top of the pack the number of cards corresponding to the number arrived at by the spectator, transferring them to the bottom of the pack. The spectator is then instructed to take the top card of the pack, to note it secretly, and not to reveal it either to you or any other spectator. He or she should then place the card face-down on top of the pack.

7. If more than four spectators are to be involved in the trick you should go through the sequence of procedures described in paragraphs 4, 5, and 6 above again to the point at which all the spectators have taken and noted a card. The final spectator to take a card should replace it on the top of the face-down pack.

8. In handling the pack after the replacement of this card by the last spectator note the identify of the bottom card of the pack. Having done so, allow each of the spectators who are taking part in the trick to cut and complete *(For an explanation of the term "cut and complete" see the "Introduction".)* You then take the pack, turn it face-up and spread it show the mix of the cards. Note the location of your noted card and cut the pack to place this card at the bottom of the face-down pack.

9. With the pack face-down now deal out face-down onto the table as many cards as there are spectators who have taken and noted a card. Having done so, pick up the cards you have dealt out and mix them. Then, with the cards still face-down to you, hand the packet to each spectator in turn and ask them to confirm that their card is in the packet.

10. You now take the packet and spread it out face-up on the table. You instruct the spectators on your count of "1-2-3" to shout out the identity of their card and to pick it up. They will all shout out and attempt to pick up the same Ace.

"OLD WINE IN A NEW BOTTLE"

T HERE ARE SOME CARD TRICKS that can be described as "classic" either because the outcome of the trick is well-known to the audience (for example, where a spectator thinks of a card and the performer then produces or names the thought-of card) or because the trick is of a particular genre (for example, where the location of a card in the pack or deck is discovered by spelling out the name of the card). What this chapter does is to take a number of these "classic" tricks and, by adapting them, produce a much heightened effect in each case.

The chapter sets out the complete instructions for the performance of a routine using these tricks. Only a minimum of skill in card manipulation is required to perform the routine and such manipulations as are required are fully explained and described. In addition, complete instructions for the performance of any sleights-of-hand referred to in the text are given—although the routine can be performed without the use of any as the tricks are self-working, the sleights-of-hand being used only to heighten the appearance of the cards being indiscriminately mixed. The basic routine, which can be readily adapted to suit any circumstances, lasts for approximately 25 minutes.

Preparation

To perform the routine you require two packs of cards of identical design but with different coloured backs. For the purposes of description it will be assumed that one pack has Blue-backed cards and that the other pack is Red-backed—but any two colours are suitable.

The routine has as its foundation two tricks where the cards in the pack have been arranged (or "*stacked*") before the performance to produce particular outcomes. In addition, if you choose to use a bridged card to control the cutting of the pack you must produce such a card for each of the packs. (*A definition of what is meant by a "bridged card" is given in the "Introduction".*) You should note, however, that the tricks can be performed without the use of such a card and details of how this is done are given with the instructions for the individual tricks in the relevant chapters.

If you do choose to produce bridged cards for each of the packs they should be given a **convex** bridge along their length, ie. the pressure to produce the bridge should be applied to the sides of the cards producing an outward curve to the face of the card. Any of the 52 cards in the pack may be bridged, but preferably the card should be easily recognised and remembered by the performer. A suitable card for a Blue-backed pack would be the King of Spades (KS) and for a Red-backed pack a suitable card would be the Queen of Diamonds (QD). Only a very light bridge is required to produce the necessary effect and instructions on how to create such a bridge and how to use the card in the handling of the pack are set out in the relevant section of the chapter on *"Handling and Sleights-of-Hand"*.

Having produced the bridged cards you can now move on to the arrangement of the packs for the first two tricks of the routine.

Begin by arranging (or "stacking") the Blue-backed pack or the pack you intend to use for the trick *"Think of a Card—Spell Another"*. To do this you require in addition to the 52 cards of the pack four **identical** Joker cards with the same pattern and colour backs and four blank-faced cards with the same backs. The Joker cards in the Waddington *"No 1"* packs (both Bridge-size packs and the Poker-size packs) are identical and as such would require you to obtain only two packs of either size to produce four identical Joker cards. In the other packs the Joker cards differ (being either of a different design or one being "red" and the other "black") so to produce four identical Joker cards you would need to obtain four packs. With regard to the blank-faced cards these can be purchased for the *"Bicycle Rider Back"* pack and for the Piatnik *"Classic"* pack but you will need to make them yourself if you intend to use either the Waddington or the W.H. Smith pack. This can be done using self-adhesive address labels trimmed to size. It might be thought the finish and handling of such doctored cards would attract attention and suspicion but you will see when you come to study the details of the trick in which they are used that this is not so.

Having obtained your four identical Blue-backed Joker cards and your four Blue-backed blank faced cards proceed to arrange the Blue-backed pack:

a. The pack is arranged face-down. (Top) Joker—any 17 cards—Joker—any 8 cards and a bridged card (or any 8 cards if you are not using a bridged card)

– 6C – 10C – AC – 2C – AH – 10H – 2H – JC – JH – JS – 4S – 5H – 8S – QS – QH – 3S – KD – 5D – JD – 9D – 3D – 7D – 8D – QD – any 2 cards (or any 3 cards if you are not using a bridged card).

b. Place the arranged pack in the appropriate carton and put it aside.

You will have left out of the carton two identical Blue-backed Joker cards and four Blue-backed blank-faced cards which you will need later.

You can now turn your attention to pre-arranging (or "stacking") the Red-backed pack. Before you begin make sure that you have four Red-backed Joker cards (they do not need to be identical) and four Red-backed blank-faced cards. Then begin to pre-arrange the pack as follows:

c. Separate the 52 cards of the pack and order each suit with the cards face-down as follows:

Hearts/Diamonds:
Top: 3 – 8 – 7 – A – Q – 6 – 4 – 2 – J – K – 10 – 9 – 5

Spades/Clubs:
Top: 2 – K – 10 – Q – 7 – 3 – 4 – 9 – 5 – A – 6 – 8 – J

d. Riffle shuffle Hearts into Spades, ensuring that 5H is the bottom card of the riffled packet. (*For an explanation of how this is done, see the relevant section in the chapter "Handling and Sleights-of-Hand".*)

e. Riffle shuffle Diamonds into Clubs ensuring that JC is the bottom card of the riffled packet.

f. Place two of the Red-backed Joker cards beneath the 5H and then place the Hearts/Spades riffled packet on top of the other riffled packet.

g. Place the arranged pack in the appropriate carton and put it aside.

You should now have left two identical Blue-backed Jokers, two Red-backed Jokers, four Blue-backed blank-faced cards and four Red-backed blank-faced cards. Thoroughly mix them and place them between the two cartons of cards.

The two packs are now arranged (or "stacked") ready for the first two tricks of the routine described.

The Routine

Probably the best piece of advice that can be given with regard to card magic is to learn and know a small number of tricks thoroughly rather than a great number of tricks superficially. And the next best piece of advice is that the tricks once learned should be used within a set framework. The first piece of advice ensures that the actual performance of the tricks becomes an almost automatic operation, allowing the performer to concentrate his or her attention on the presentation of the effect. The advantages that accrue from the second piece of advice are that any pressure or distraction in having to decide during the performance what comes next is removed and the tricks can be pre-ordered in such a way as to build on each other.

The information set out in this chapter is a basis on which the courses of action recommended above can be achieved. Firstly, it provides a grouping of tricks from which the routine can be derived and the routine can be as short or as long as the circumstances of the performance require. Secondly, it provides a framework that, although pre-ordered, still allows flexibility when that is desirable.

If you examine the general overview of the routine set out on the opposite page you will see that it has as its foundation two tricks where the cards in the packs have been arranged in a particular order (or "stacked") before the performance to produce a particular effect and that each effect is related to a particular colour indicated by the colour of the back of the pack. In addition there are four other blocks of tricks and you will note that these blocks contain tricks that can be performed with any pack of cards. It is thus possible to begin a routine with either one of the tricks which depend for their effect on the pre-arrangement of the pack and to follow this trick, using the same pack, with a series of tricks which require no pre-arrangement of the pack. In doing so you are lessening the likelihood that the spectators will suspect that the pack was initially stacked, even more so, if, before it was used, it was cut or mixed as explained in the appropriate section of the chapter on *"Handling and Sleights-of-Hand."*

A General Overview

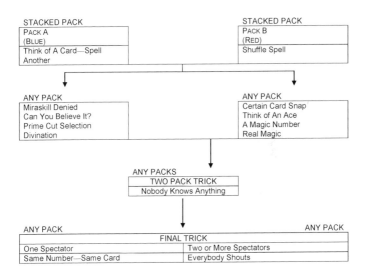

STACKED PACK		STACKED PACK	
PACK A		PACK B	
(BLUE)		(RED)	
Think of A Card—Spell Another		Shuffle Spell	

ANY PACK	ANY PACK
Miraskill Denied	Certain Card Snap
Can You Believe It?	Think of An Ace
Prime Cut Selection	A Magic Number
Divination	Real Magic

ANY PACKS
TWO PACK TRICK
Nobody Knows Anything

ANY PACK	ANY PACK
FINAL TRICK	
One Spectator	Two or More Spectators
Same Number—Same Card	Everybody Shouts

This is the basis on which the routine is built and an example will serve to show the flexibility available to suit any circumstances.

The performance begins with the two packs in their cartons on the table and with the mixed packet of Joker cards and blank-faced cards at the side of them.

Given that the spectators do not know what trick is connected with which title or pack (**and they never should**) the routine begins as follows:

"Now, I have some amazing tricks to show you:

The first is ALMOST IMPOSSIBLE.
The second is IMPOSSIBLE.

The third is EVEN MORE IMPOSSIBILE.

The fourth is THE MOST IMPOSSIBLE CARD TRICK IN THE WORLD.

And the fifth is BEYOND THE IMPOSSIBLE.

Now, which one would you like first? (The spectators choose)

And which pack would you like me to do it with? (The spectators choose)

Right—here we go."

You now perform the trick associated with the pre-arranged pack they have chosen and then continue the routine as follows:

"Well, you've had that trick—which one do you want next?

(You list the remaining "impossible" tricks and the spectators choose)

And which pack do you want me to use?"

If the spectators choose the pack you have just used for the first trick you go immediately into the first trick of any of the "four-trick any-pack" blocks. If the spectators choose the second pre-arranged pack you perform the trick associated with that pack.

The situation now is that you have performed two "impossible" tricks—either two pre-arranged tricks or one trick with a pre-arranged pack and one any-pack trick. You then proceed with further any-pack tricks to complete the sequence of five "impossible" tricks. If the spectators have chosen only one of the pre-arranged packs you will have performed all the tricks with that one pre-arranged pack. However, at any point at which the spectators choose the other pre-arranged pack you will perform the trick associated with that pack. In any case, you perform the sequence of five "impossible" tricks.

If you then wish to extend the performance you suggest that you use both packs and proceed to the "two-pack trick" and / or, if you think it appropriate, you may complete the performance with "just one final trick".

All of this then is the framework on which you can build a routine that suits you and the circumstances of the occasion.

Initially, you should concentrate your efforts on mastering the two tricks using the pre-arranged packs and one block of "four-trick any-pack" tricks. Thus you will have at your disposal from the very beginning a routine of up to six tricks based on the two pre-arranged packs (enough for most occasions), and if you are suddenly handed a pack of cards and asked to perform, you have up to four tricks immediately available. This is the firm base on which you can extend to the full repertoire of thirteen tricks.

One final observation: learn and perform the tricks in the "four-trick any-pack" blocks in the order in which they are given. There are two reasons for this. The first is that in doing so you will find them easier to remember and when performing you will be relieved of the pressure of deciding what trick to do next. The second is that they are ordered in such a way that one trick leads naturally into the next and in the case of *"Miraskill Denied"* and *"Can You Believe It"* the first trick sets up the cards to allow you to perform the second trick.

Now, armed with your two packs and with the tricks you have perfected you are ready to produce some magic with the cards.

So, on to the tricks, beginning with the pre-arranged tricks.

The Pre-Arranged Tricks

"Blue Pack"—
"Think of A Card—Spell Another"

Effect

Cards are dealt randomly to produce four 8-card hands. Each spectator has a free choice of any one of these hands from which they mentally select one card each. Eventually, they spell out their thought-of card from another 8-card packet without revealing the card. When the two cards are revealed they discover they have spelled out each other's card.

Performance

1. You begin by asking a spectator to sort out the four Blue-backed blank-faced cards from the eight blank-faced cards and the two Blue-backed Joker cards from the four Joker cards. You take these cards and place them in front of yourself. The Red-backed blank-faced cards and Joker cards you place aside.

2. You now take the Blue-backed carton and take out the cards, taking care not to disturb the order of the cards. Having done so, you perform a false cut followed by a false mix of the pack (*see the relevant sections in the chapter on "Handling and Sleights-of-Hand"*). If you choose not to perform these moves you merely place the pack face-down on the table.

3. Explain that to perform the trick you require four Joker cards so you will need to extract the two Joker cards from the pack. However, rather than just going through it to find them, you "will try a little magic".

4. Invite a spectator to cut off about the top half of the pack and place it face-down on the table. Point out that as there are two Joker cards in the pack there will be 54 cards in the pack and that half the pack would be 27 cards. Pick up the packet the spectator has placed on the table and count it out face-down into a pile on the table. (*In doing this you are reversing the order of the cards—see the definition of "counting the cards reversing their order" in the "Introduction".*)

5. If on the count you have 27 cards, well and good. If you have more than 27 cards stop the counting at 27 and return the extra cards to the top of the other half of the pack without reversing their order. If you have less than 27 cards in the count make up the number by taking cards off the top of the other half of the pack one at a time and placing them on the face-down pile.

6. Take the cards you have counted out and neaten up the pile. Then instruct the spectator to cut the pile roughly in half and to keep the cards he or she has cut off. You take the bottom part of the pile and place it to one side.

7. Now instruct the spectator **to deal** out the cards he or she has into a face-down pile on the table, counting them as he or she does so. Take the number arrived at and add the two digits of the numbers together to give a single digit number (ie. 14 = 1 + 4 = 5). The spectator then takes the pile of cards from the table, counts down in the pile to the card at that number placing each card face-down in a pile on the table. He or she then takes the card at the top of the cards of the packet from which he or she is counting and places it face-down in front of him- or herself. You take the cards that the spectator has left, pick up the pile you placed aside at paragraph 6, and place these cards on top of the cards you have taken from the spectator. You then place this

combined packet below the cards that the spectator counted off and then place all the cards on top of the other "half" of the pack.

8. You now repeat the procedure set out in paragraphs 4-7 to find the second Joker. However, this time *you count only 26 cards*.

9. Turn over the two face-down cards. They are the two Joker cards you required. Confirm that as you now have four Joker cards you can "get on with the trick".

10. Take the packet you re-constituted at paragraph 8 and ask the spectator whether he or she wishes it to be placed on top or at the bottom of the cards you put aside at paragraph 6. Do as the spectator wishes, pointing out that this now gives you a complete pack of 52 cards. Place the pack face-down in front of yourself on the table. (*If you are using a bridged card to control the cutting of the cards you should note that this card was the top card of the cards you put aside at paragraph 6. If you are not using a bridged card you should glimpse and remember the identity of the card which is at the bottom of the reconstituted packet from paragraph 7.*)

11. You now take the four Joker cards and place them face-down on the table as the bottom cards of what will be four separate face-down piles.

12. Now turn the pack face-up and spread it to show the mix of the cards. Having done so, you turn it face down and cut and complete (*for a definition of "cut and complete" see the "Introduction"*). You then invite the spectators to cut and complete, at will. Finally, you cut the bridged card to the bottom of the pack or if you are not using a bridged card you turn the pack face-up and spread it to show the mix of the cards—as you do so you split the pack at the card above the card you

noted at paragraph 10 and take this card and all the cards below it to the bottom of the pack—you then turn the pack face-down.

13. You begin to deal out the pack placing a card face-down in turn onto each of the face-down Joker cards taking instructions from the spectators as to the order in which the cards are placed. In other words, you will deal out 24 cards—one in turn onto each Joker card, the order of dealing in each four-card group being determined by the spectators. You continue until you have dealt out six cards onto each Joker card. As you deal each card you show it to the spectators telling them that eventually they are going to have to note and remember one of them. (*You do not look at the cards yourself—unless there is only one spectator in which case you are acting in place of a second spectator.*)

14. When the deal is completed place a blank-faced card face-down—one on each pile of face-down cards.

15. You now invite the spectator or the spectators to decide which piles will be paired. (*The trick will work for any two hands.*)

16. When this has been done you pick up each pile in turn and deal them out face-down onto the table, showing each card in turn to the spectator whose pile it is. This, you tell him or her, is to allow him or her to see the cards again and this time to select one mentally and to remember it. You point out that they may, if they wish, select the "*Joker Card*" or "*The Invisible Card*" (ie. the blank-faced card). (*In doing this you are, in fact, reversing the order of the cards into the order required to perform the trick. You place the cards face-down in each pile not looking at them yourself—unless you are acting as a second spectator. In which case the pile you look at will be Pile B—see paragraph 18.*)

17. The piles are now treated in pairs between the spectators or between you and one spectator. Each pair is handled separately as a pair as described below.

18. Treat each pair as A and B (A left; B right). In picking up the piles place A on B and then place the pair you intend to deal with first (or in the case of only one spectator his or her pile and your pile) on top of the other pair. You then place all these cards face-down on the top or at the bottom of the rest of the pack as instructed by the spectator. (*You should note that if you are using a bridged card then this card is now in place to allow the spectators to cut and complete at will. If you are not using a bridged card then the card you noted at paragraph 10 will serve the same purpose.*)

19. The spectator or spectators are now invited to cut and complete the pack, at will. Finally, if you are using a bridged card you cut that card to the bottom of the pack. If you are not using a bridged card you spread the cards as described at paragraph 12 and this time split the pack **at the card noted at paragraph 10**.

20. Deal out the cards face-down to produce either two 8-card hands or four 8-card hands as appropriate, ensuring that the spectator receives the first hand dealt if there is only one spectator or the spectators receive A and B as they examined the cards to memorise them (A left; B right). The cards are dealt **consecutively** (*see the "Introduction" for a definition of this term*) A and B for the first two hands and then A and B for the second two hands (*Note: these are A and B as they are dealt from the pack*).

21. Take each packet and show the cards in it to the appropriate spectator dealing them out face-down onto the table. Ask the spectator if they see their card in the packet. You do not look at the face of the card

unless you are acting as a second spectator (*Note: the dealing has reversed the order of the cards which is what is required for the mechanism of the trick.*)

22. Proceed as follows depending upon the answers:

    a. Both answer "Yes" or both answer "No"
        Place B on A
    b. One answers "Yes" the other "No"
        Place A on B

23. Now place the packet (or the two packets in appropriate order) on the top of the pack (which has the bridged card or the card noted at paragraph 10 as its bottom card) and proceed as described at paragraph 19.

24. Now repeat paragraphs 20-23 **TWO** more times.

25. You are now going into the final deal to produce the 8-card hands from which the spectators will spell out their cards. To do this proceed as follows: *Deal* off (face-down) in front of yourself A and B (dealing a card **consecutively** to each hand). Invite the spectator who has been receiving A throughout the trick to choose one of the two hands. If the spectator chooses A give it to him or her and instruct him or her to give it to the other spectator. If the spectator chooses B give that hand to him or her and the other hand (A) to the other spectator. In any case, "Spectator A" gets B and "Spectator B" gets A.

26. Now take each packet in turn and deal it out as described at paragraph 21. Ask the spectators if they see their card (their answers are immaterial). Hand the packets back to them and instruct them, in turn, to spell out (silently) their memorised card and to place the appropriate card (unseen) face-down in front of themselves on the table. (*If you are acting as the second spectator you should*

state your card and spell it out first.) The method of spelling to be used, which you can demonstrate using what is left of the pack, is as follows:

a. The top card of the face-down packet is taken to the bottom of the packet as the first letter, the second card is taken to the bottom of the packet as the second letter . . . and so on.

b. The spelling is "A – C – E – O – F – C – L – U – B – S", "N – I – N – E – O – F – H – E – A – R – T – S", etc.

c. The card to be taken is the card arrived at on the final "S" of the suit.

d. However, *you must stress*

"*J – O – K – E – R – C – A – R – D*"
and
"*T – H – E – I – N – V – I – S – I – B –
L – E – C – A – R – D*" and the card to be taken is at the final "D" of "C – A – R – D".

If you are in any doubt about the spectator's ability to complete this successfully then have them state their cards and guide them through it.

27. When the spelling is complete ask the spectators what card they were thinking of. When the cards are turned over they will find that in each pair they have arrived at the other's card. (If you are acting as a second spectator you will have arrived at the spectator's card and the spectator will have arrived at your card.)

"Red Pack"—"Shuffle Spell"

Effect

The pack is cut and shuffled after which a spectator is asked to choose any suit. This suit is extracted from the pack. The spectator is then asked to choose either of the suits of the opposite colour and this suit is extracted from the pack. These two suits are now shuffled together and the spectator is asked which suit he or she wishes to have. The appropriate suit is then dealt to him or her and the other suit is dealt out to the performer. It is obvious to the spectator that the two packets are in totally different random orders. A spelling out then proceeds whereby one packet spells out the cards as they are turned over from the other packet. Finally, the performer, using a suit chosen by the spectator, spells out any card in that suit thought of by the spectator.

Performance

1. Pick up the Red-backed carton and take out the cards, taking care not to disturb the order of the cards. Having done so you perform a false cut of the pack (*see the relevant section in the chapter on "Handling and Sleights-of-Hand"*). If you choose not to perform this move you merely place the pack face-down on the table.

2. Explain that you will need to extract the Joker cards from the pack. (*NOTE: They are in the middle of the pack.*) To do this turn the pack face-up and spread it out until the Joker cards appear. Take them out and place

them aside. In doing this keep the two packets that were divided by the Joker cards separate. You now turn over the two packets and riffle shuffle them into each other. (*For details of how to perform a riffle shuffle see the relevant section in the chapter on "Handling and Sleights-of-Hand"*). In performing the spread and the extraction of the Joker cards you should perform the move quickly as, although the cards are mixed in value and colour, a slow spread might allow a keen-eyed spectator to observe that only two suits are present in each of the packets.

3. Having riffle shuffled the packets together invite the spectator to choose any suit. Once he or she has done so turn the pack face-up and go through the pack extracting the cards of this suit which should be placed in a face-up pile on the table. The other cards are also placed in a face-up pile on the table. In doing this do not disturb the order of the cards, ie. place the cards one on top of the other as they come out of the pack.

4. You now ask the spectator to choose a suit of the opposite colour. When he or she has done so pick up the other cards and repeat the procedure of extraction of the suit as described at paragraph 3. You then turn face-down the pile of cards of the non-selected suits and place them to one side.

5. Take the two piles of face-up cards, turn them face-down and riffle shuffle them into each other.

6. You now invite the spectators to say which colour suit he or she wishes to have. When he or she has done so, turn the packet face-up and deal out the cards into two face-up piles—the selected suit to the spectator and the other suit to yourself. In doing so do not disturb the order of the cards, ie. place them one on top of the other as they come out of the face-up packet.

7. In order for you to now bring the trick to its conclusion, you must know how it is structured. You have on the table two piles of face-up cards—one of a red suit and the other of a black suit. You should note that the black suit, using the spelling-out system to be described later, will spell out the cards of the red suit as they are turned over but you should also note that this will only be achieved if the top card of the red pile when that pile is turned face-down is the 3, and when the top card of the black pile when that pile is turned face down is the 2. What you must now do therefore is to arrange the cards in this way. This is done on the subterfuge of establishing that both you and the spectator have all the thirteen cards of the appropriate suit. You do this by counting each pile in turn. If the cards of the pile are correctly configured you count the pile without reversing the order of the cards (*see the relevant section in the "Introduction"*). If the cards of the pile are **not** correctly configured you count the cards reversing their order. Having done this you place each pile face down on the table—the appropriate pile in front of the spectator and the other pile in front of yourself.

8. If the spectator has the red suit instruct him or her to turn over the first card on the top of the pile in front of him- or herself and to place it face-up on the table by the side of the pile (*NOTE: It should be the 3*). You then pick up your pile and spell out the value of the card ("T-H-R-E-E") and for each letter you transfer a card face-down (unseen) from the top to the bottom of your packet. You then take the top card of the packet, turn it over and place it face-up in front of yourself. It will be the 3. You go through the piles repeating this process. In each case you will spell out the card turned over

by the spectator and you will each finish with a pile of face-up cards in front of you.

9. If at paragraph 8 **you** have the red suit turn over the first card on the top of your pile and place it face-up on the table by the side of your pile. (*NOTE: It should be the 3*). You then instruct the spectator to pick up his or her pile and to spell out the value of the card ("T-H-R-E-E") using the spelling system described at paragraph 8. He or she will spell out the card turned over by you and you will each finish with a pile of face-up cards in front of you.

10. You may if you wish finish the trick at this point but, if you choose to do so, you may extend it as follows:

a. The two face-up piles on the table are so configured that if you pick up any one of them, turn it face down, and spell out the cards from Ace to King in that order using the spelling system described at paragraph 8 you will spell out the suit in sequence.

b. You may therefore now invite the spectator to think of any card in either of the suits. When he or she has done so pick up the two piles and, after turning them face down, riffle shuffle them into each other.

c. You now ask the spectator to declare the suit of the thought-of card.

d. When the spectator has done so you pick up the face-down riffled packet and, with the faces of the cards towards you and the back of the cards towards the spectator, you go through the packet placing the cards of the declared suit face-up in a pile on the table and the cards of the other suit (without showing them) face-down in a pile on the table, in the order in which they come out of the packet.

e.   Now on the subterfuge of confirming that you have all thirteen cards of the suit you count them reversing their order and then turn the packet face-down.

f.   You take the face-down packet and begin to spell out the cards from Ace through to King, using the spelling-out procedure described at paragraph 8. At each appropriate card you take the card from the top of the pack, without revealing it, and place it face-down, forming a face-down pile on the table. Instruct the spectator to inform you when you have spelled out the value of his or her thought-of card. When he or she does so and when you turn the card at the top of the face-down pile over it will be the spectator's thought-of card.

The Any-Pack Tricks

"Miraskill Denied"

EFFECT

The pack is thoroughly shuffled. The performer then demonstrates that if a pack is dealt out in pairs there is an almost certain probability that there will be a number of like pairs (ie. Red/Red and Black/Black) in the dealing and that the number of Red pairs will equal the number of Black pairs. The performer does this with fewer and fewer cards until from a very small packet the performer produces one red pair and one black pair. He or she then takes the whole pack, shuffles it, shows the mix of the pack, and states that he or she will perform the almost impossible feat of dealing out the whole pack without producing a single like pair. This the performer then proceeds to do.

PERFORMANCE

1. By way of introducing the trick inform the spectators that a classic trick developed by a card magician in the 1930s (Stewart James) was given the name *"Miraskill"* and is based on the observation that if you take a pack of cards, shuffle it, and deal it out in pairs of cards, there is an almost certain probability that you will produce an equal number of red and black pairs.

2. Proceed to demonstrate that this is so by shuffling the pack, allowing the spectator to shuffle the pack, and by then inviting the spectator to deal out the pack in pairs of cards. (*NOTE: Your shuffle should be a riffle shuffle—see the relevant section in the chapter on*

"Handling and Sleights-of-Hand" for how to perform a riffle shuffle. The spectator may shuffle or mix the cards as he or she wishes.)

3. The spectator should take the face-down pack and turn over the cards in pairs from the top of the pack. The like pairs should be placed face-up on the table—the Red/Red in one pile and the Black/Black in a second pile. Any unlike pairs should be handed to you. As you take these cards separate them one to each hand, ostensibly to show off a red card and a black card. However, as you bring them together ensure that you order them so that when you turn them face-down and place them on a discard pile the red card will be the top card of the pair. Do this quickly while encouraging the spectator in his or her dealing out of the pairs. (*NOTE: What you are doing is to make up a face-down discard pile which consists of unlike pairs in the sequence Red/ Black Red/Black etc throughout the pile.*)

4. When the dealing out is completed invite the spectator to confirm that he or she has an equal number of black and red pairs. (*NOTE: In the very unlikely event that no pairs have been produced (**which is very, very unlikely**) express your surprise, and suggest that the spectator takes out a subscription to a lottery, and repeat paragraphs 2-4.*)

5. Invite the spectator to shuffle together or thoroughly mix the cards he or she has counted out. Take the shuffled packet, turn it face-up, and spread it to show the mix. In splitting it into two packets for a riffle shuffle ensure that the bottom card of each packet is of the same colour. Then riffle shuffle the two packets together, ensuring that in the shuffle the bottom cards of each packet drop together. (*NOTE: This **guarantees** that*

there will be at least one red pair and one black pair in the dealing out of the packet.)

6. Point out that there are now fewer cards but that the probability of producing like pairs from it is still very high. Hand the packet to the spectator and instruct him or her to repeat the procedure set out at paragraph 3. Again, you deal with the unlike pairs as described in paragraph 3.

7. Continue the procedure set out at paragraphs 2-6. As the packet reduces to very few cards it is advisable that you not only shuffle the cards but that you also turn over the pairs of cards yourself. Continue the procedure until only one red pair and one black pair is produced. Take these pairs and, in turning them face down to place them on the discard pile, ensure that the red cards slide into the black cards to produce a Red-Black-Red-Black sequence when the cards are placed face-down on the pile.

8. Now take the discard pile and mix it using a Charlier Shuffle (*see the relevant section in the chapter on "Handling and Sleights-of-Hand" for how to perform this shuffle*). Then allow the spectator to cut and complete the pack, at will (*for a definition of the term "cut and complete" see the "Introduction"*).

9. You now Charlier Shuffle again and then finally allow the spectator to cut and complete the pack. When the cutting has been completed you pick up the face-down pack and, with the faces of the cards towards yourself and the back of the cards towards the spectator, you divide the pack into two packets, ensuring that the face cards (ie. the bottom cards of the packets when they are face-down) are of a different colour. You then turn the packets face-down and riffle shuffle one packet into the other.

10. Having done this turn the pack face-up and spread it to show the mix of the cards. While you are doing this you declare that you will now guarantee to do something that is all-nigh impossible, ie. that you will deal out the pack in pairs without producing a single like pair.

11. You proceed to do so handling the cards as described below:

    a.   From the face-down packs turn the cards face-up in pairs and rest them on top of the face-down pack.

    b.   If the red card is the top face-up card of the pair move that card slightly away from the pack, place the black card on top of it and then place both cards face-down on the table, declaring "a red and a black" as the base of a face-down pile.

    c.   If the black card is the top face-up card of the pair push the red card from beneath it away from the pack and slide the black card on top of it before placing both cards face-down on the table, declaring "a black and a red".

12. You will go through the pack producing only unlike pairs. (*NOTE: You are also producing a face-down pack with the cards arranged in such a way as is required for the trick "Can You Believe It?"*)

"Can You Believe It?"

EFFECT

The pack is thoroughly mixed and cut by the performer and the spectators. Each of two spectators is then dealt two face-down cards from which each secretly selects one card. The cards are returned to the pack which is shuffled and cut. The cards are then dealt out into four piles, alternating face-up and face-down, producing a pile of red face-up cards, a pile of black face-up cards, and two piles of face-down cards. Each spectator is handed a pile of face-up cards and a pile of face-down cards and instructed to shuffle them together to produce a face-down packet. Each spectator then deals out their shuffled packet face-up to produce a pile of cards that are all of one colour except for one card which is of the opposite colour. The card of the opposite colour will be their selected card.

PERFORMANCE

(NOTE: This trick depends for its successful outcome on the use of the pack from the performance of the trick "Miraskill Denied". It does not need to follow that trick immediately but, when it is performed, the order of the cards from the conclusion of "Miraskill Denied" must not have been disturbed.)

1.   Take the pack in the order it was left at the conclusion of the trick *"Miraskill Denied"* and give it a Charlier Shuffle or mix *(see the relevant section in the chapter*

on "Handling and Sleights-of-Hand" for how to perform this shuffle). Then allow the spectators to cut and complete the pack, at will (*for a definition of the term "cut and complete" see the "Introduction"*).

2. You now Charlier Shuffle again and then finally allow the spectators to cut and complete the pack, at will. When the cutting has been completed you pick up the face-down pack and, with the faces of the cards towards yourself and the backs of the cards towards the spectators, you note the colour of the bottom card of the pack.

3. Now deal off the top of the **face-down** pack two cards **face-down** to each spectator. Deal out the cards as indicated below:

Spectator A		Spectator B	
1	3	2	4

(If there is only one spectator available you should act as Spectator B.)

(*NOTE: Spectator A now has two cards of the same colour and the colour is the opposite colour to that of the card at the bottom of the pack. Spectator B (or you if you are acting as the second spectator) also has two cards of the same colour—in this case the same colour as that of the card at the bottom of the pack.*)

4. Instruct each spectator to choose either one of the two cards they have and to take it and note it secretly. (*If you are acting as the second spectator you should note one of your two cards*). While this is being done you should return the two cards not chosen to the top of the pack in the order of Spectator B's card first and Spectator

A's card second, ie. Spectator A's card is the top card of the face-down pack.

5. You now invite Spectator B to place his or her noted card face-down on top of the pack—and then likewise Spectator A.

6. Immediately, cut the pack into two roughly equal packets, ensuring that on splitting the pack the two packets have different coloured bottom cards. You now riffle shuffle the two packets together, this time ensuring that the top two cards of the pack remain as the top two cards of the riffled pack. (*For details of how this is done, see the relevant section in the chapter on "Handling and Sleights-of-Hand"*).

7. Now deal out two cards face-down from the top of the face-down pack. They should be dealt thus:

   Position 1   Position 2

   (*NOTE: The card at Position 1 is Spectator A's chosen card of which you know the colour and the card at Position 2 is Spectator B's chosen card which is of the opposite colour.*)

8. You continue dealing out from the top of the face-down pack in a procedure that appears complicated on first-reading but which you will find extremely straight-forward once you have gone through it with the cards. The procedure is as follows:

   a. Turn the next card you take from the top of the pack face-up. If it is the same colour that you know Spectator A's card is, place it at Position 4. If it is the opposite colour to that you know Spectator A's card is place it at Position 3.

Position 1   Position 2
Position 3   Position 4

b. Take the next card from the top of the pack face-down and place it face-down on the face-down card at the diagonal to which you placed the face-up card, ie. if you placed the face-up card at Position 3 the face-down card is placed at Position 2; if you placed the face-up card at Position 4 the face-down card is placed at Position 1.

c. Turn the next card from the top of the pack face-up. You will have a face-up card at either Position 3 or Position 4. If the card you have taken from the top of the pack is the same colour as the face-up card on the table place it face-up on the top of that card. If the card you have taken from the pack is the opposite colour to the face-up card on the table place it face-up at the unoccupied position.

d. Take the next card from the top of the pack face-down and place it face-down on the face-down card at the diagonal to which you placed the face-up card.

e. Continue in this way through the pack placing face-up cards on the appropriately coloured face-up card position and the following face-down card face-down at the diagonal position.

f. The end result is that you now have on the table:

Position 1: Face-down cards (all of one colour) and Spectator A's selected card of a different colour, (also face-down).

Position 2: Face-down cards (all of one
colour) and Spectator B's card of a
different colour, (also face down).

Position 3: Face-up cards (all of one colour)
and different in colour to Spectator A's
selected card.

Position 4: Face-up cards (all of one colour)
and different in colour to Spectator B's
selected card.

9. Hand the cards at Position 3 to Spectator A and instruct
him or her to turn them face-down and shuffle them into
the already face-down cards at Position 1.

10. Hand the cards at Position 4 to Spectator B and instruct
him or her to do likewise with the cards at Position 2
(or, if you are acting as Spectator B you perform this
procedure).

11. Having done this each spectator should turn their
packets face-up and either spread out the cards or deal
out the cards. They will each find that they have all the
cards of the pack of one colour except one which will
be of the opposite colour—and the card of the opposite
colour will be their selected card. (*NOTE: If you are
acting as Spectator B you should allow Spectator A to
go first before you declare your selected card and turn
over your packet.*)

"Prime Cut Selection"

Effect

A spectator is given a completely free choice of card which he or she secretly notes and returns to the pack. The spectator then cuts a packet from the pack. Using this packet the performer deals a packet of cards from it and invites the spectator to select any number he or she wishes `from 1 to the number of cards in the packet. Using that number the performer proceeds to eliminate cards in the packet finishing with one face-down card which proves to be the spectator's selected card.

Performance

1. Allow the spectator to shuffle the pack and to cut it, at will. Take the pack and shuffle it yourself—finally cutting the bridged card to the bottom of the pack. If you choose not to use a bridged card you should glimpse and note the identity of the bottom card of the pack after your shuffle.

2. Invite the spectator to cut off three approximately equal packets from the top of the face-down pack, to choose one of the packets, and from that packet to choose any card, which he or she should secretly note.

3. When the spectator has selected his or her card take all the other cards and place them on top of what was the bottom part of the pack, ensuring that either the bridged card or your noted card remains at the bottom of the pack.

4. Now allow the spectator to return the selected card to the pack—on the top, or the bottom, or in the "middle", using the bridged card to bring the selected card to the top of the pack (*for details on how to do this see the relevant section in the chapter on "Handling and Sleights-of-Hand"*). If you are not using a bridged card allow the spectator to replace his or her selected card on either the top or the bottom of the pack and to then cut and complete the pack (*for an explanation of the term "cut and complete" see the "Introduction"*). When the cutting is completed take the pack, holding it so that the faces of the cards are towards you and the backs of the cards are towards the spectator. Split the pack at the point in the pack where you see your noted card and then turn the two packets face-down. One packet will have your noted card as the bottom card, the other will have the selected card as its top card. You may then either place the packet with your noted card beneath the other packet or you may riffle shuffle the two packets into each other, ensuring that the top card of the packet not containing your noted card drops as the top card of the riffled pack (*for details on how to do this see the relevant section of the chapter on "Handling and Sleights-of-Hand*).

5. Place the pack face-down on the table and invite the spectator to cut off a packet of cards from the top of the pack. This packet he or she hands to you.

6. Deal out face-down from the top of the packet seven cards and then pause. Ask the spectator if he or she wishes you to deal any more cards. If the answer is "yes" deal off a further four cards—and pause again. Repeat the question—if the answer is again "yes" deal off a further two cards.

7. You now have seven, eleven, or thirteen cards in a face-down pile on the table. Pick up the packet and count it out without reversing the order of the cards (*see the "Introduction" for details on how to do this*).

8. With the packet face-down ask the spectator to select any number from 1 up to and including the number of cards in the packet. Once the spectator has done so you then proceed to reveal the selected card using the procedure set out below.

   a. Using the spectator's chosen number, say 4, take off in turn cards from the top of the face-down packet and, without revealing them, place them face down at the bottom of the packet. With the 4th card (ie. the final card) turn it face-up and then place it at the bottom of the packet.

   b. Count again four cards off the top of the pack as in paragraph 8a above.

   c. Continue with this process taking both face-up and face-down cards until there is only one face-down card left in the packet. This will be the spectator's selected card.

   If the spectator chooses 1 as the number count out "1" and slide the bottom card away from the packet. Turn it face-up and place it on top of the packet. If the spectator chooses the total number of cards in the packet as the number count out that total transferring cards *face-down* to the bottom of the packet and then turn the packet face-up to reveal the card.

"Divination"

Effect

The pack is divided into two packets—one packet consisting of the red cards, the other all the black cards. The spectator is invited to choose any one of the packets, the performer takes the other packet. The performer then declares that the trick requires that both the performer and the spectator have an equal number of like pairs. The spectator determines how many pairs each will have and these are sorted out from the packets. After a series of shuffles and cuts the two series of pairs are dealt out—one to the spectator and one to the performer. The packets receive one final cut. The performer then takes a card from the spectator's face-up packet and places it on the table face-up (say, a 6). The spectator now takes any card he or she wishes from their face-up packet and places it face-up on the table (say, a 9). These two numbers are then added together (ie. 6 + 9 = 15). The performer counts out 15 cards from the face-down packet and arrives at a 9, the same value as the card selected by the spectator. The trick can be repeated as many times as the spectator or the performer wishes.

Performance

1. Begin by dividing the pack into two packets—one of all the red cards and the other of all the black. Allow the spectator to choose one of the packets.

2. Explain that the trick requires that you each have an equal number of like pairs (e.g. two Aces, two 2s, two 3s, etc) and that he or she can choose how many pairs. Point out, however, that any number from five to thirteen makes for a more interesting trick. When he or she has chosen the number, say 9—explain that each of you now needs to extract from your packet the two Aces, two 2s, two 3s, two 4s, two 5s, two 6s, two 7s, two 8s, and two 9s. If the spectator had chosen above this number you would need to go on to the two 10s, two Jacks (11), two Queens (12) and two Kings (13).

3. Instruct the spectator to extract the appropriate number of pairs from his or her packet. While the spectator is doing this you too extract the appropriate pairs. However, as you do so, you arrange the cards to provide two ascending sequences. For example with the cards at paragraph 2 above your cards would be ordered Ace – 2 – 3 – 4 – 5 – 6 – 7 – 8 – 9 – Ace – 2 – 3 – 4 – 5 – 6 – 7 – 8 – 9 when your packet was turned face down. (The positioning of the suits is immaterial.)

4. Once both you and the spectator have completed the sorting out place the unwanted cards aside and instruct the spectator to give his or her packet a good shuffle and mix.

5. You then take your face-down packet and place it on the table. Allow the spectator to cut and complete as many times as he or she wishes (*for an explanation of this term see the "Introduction"*). You pick up the packet and observe that rather than shuffle it where you will have control of the cards you will allow the spectator to determine how the cards are mixed. You then perform a Charlier Shuffle or mix allowing the spectator to determine how many cards you take at

each stage (*for details on how to perform this shuffle see the chapter on "Handling and Sleights-of-Hand"*).

6. When the Charlier Shuffle is completed allow the spectator to cut and complete the packet, at will.

7. As you pick up the packet note the bottom card—this is your key card.

8. You now ask the spectator to take his or her packet and to turn it face up and to shuffle it. You then choose a card from the face-up packet and place it face-up on the table. (*NOTE: The card you choose should be the number of the pairs each of you has* **minus** *your key card value. For example, if you each have nine pairs and the value of your key card is a 6 the card you choose will be a 3, ie. 9 - 6 = 3. If the value of your key card is a 9 the calculation would be 9 - 9 = 0 and in this case you would not choose a card but you would invite the spectator to choose any card he or she wished and use the value of that card to determine the number of cards you counted down to in your packet—see paragraphs 9-11 below.*)

9. You now invite the spectator to select any card he or she wishes from the face-up packet and place it face-up by the side of the card you have chosen. Add the value of these two cards together (with Jacks = 11, Queens = 12, Kings = 13, if these pairs have been used). Point out that in arriving at this number your card was chosen before the spectator made his or her choice. You may also, if you wish, allow the spectator to change his or her card to arrive at a different number.

10. Once the number has been arrived at replace the card you chose in the face-up packet, leaving the spectator's face-up card on the table.

11. You now count off from the top of your face-down packet cards equal in number to the number arrived at

in paragraph 9 above, taking each card as you count it to the bottom of the packet (face-down). When you arrive at the card corresponding to the number place it face-down by the side of the spectator's face-up card and instruct the spectator to turn it face-up. It will be of the same numerical value as the spectator's selected card.

12. You may, if you wish, now repeat the trick. If you choose to do so, proceed as follows:

   a. Replace the spectator's card in the face-up packet and replace your own card face-down on top of your face-down packet.

   b. As you now know the value of the top card of your packet it is possible for you to calculate the value of the bottom card of your packet, ie. it is 1 less in value than the top card—if the top card is a 4 then the bottom card is a 3. **This is your new key card.** You should note that if the top card of your packet is an Ace then the bottom card is the value of the total number of pairs in the packet, eg. if the sequences are Ace to King then the bottom card is a King (13).

   c. You now proceed to repeat the procedure described in paragraphs 8-11 above. Alternatively, you may allow the spectator to cut and complete the packet and repeat the trick beginning at paragraph 5 above.

"Certain Card Snap"

EFFECT

A spectator shuffles the pack. The performer instructs him or her to remove any four cards to reduce the pack to 48 cards. The performer shuffles these cards and counts them out face-down onto the table into six 8-card hands. Each of the spectators chooses any hand, mentally selects a card, and shuffles the cards again. The pack is re-constituted, cut by the spectators, and dealt out into eight 6-card face-down hands. The spectators examine the hands and take the hand in which they find their mentally selected card. When their hands are combined and dealt out the spectators are asked to play a form of "SNAP" in which each turns over the other's card.

PERFORMANCE

1. This trick is best performed with two spectators. However, if a second spectator is not available you may take that part.
2. Begin by inviting one of the spectators to shuffle the pack and to extract any four cards from within it to produce a 48-card pack. Place the four extracted cards aside.
3. You take the pack and shuffle it and then cut the bridged card to the bottom of the pack. If you are not using a bridged card you merely shuffle the pack.
4. You now take the pack and count, out without reversing the order of the cards, six 8-card face-down hands,

counting out each hand in turn (*see the "Introduction" for an explanation of "counting out without reversing the order of the cards"*) (*NOTE: If you are using a bridged card this procedure ensures that the bridged card is at the bottom of the last hand counted out. You should note and remember the position of this hand.*)

5. You now instruct the first spectator (Spectator A) to take any one of these hands to shuffle it, and mentally select any of the cards in the hand. He or she then shuffles the hand again and places it face-down on the table. From the five remaining hands Spectator B does the same.

6. For each of the spectators you take two of the non-selected hands and invite the spectator to place his or her hand between them. (*NOTE: If neither of the spectators has chosen the hand with the bridged card at the bottom ensure that this hand with the bridged card at the bottom is placed beneath the hand of Spectator A. If the hand with the bridged card has been chosen or if you are not using a bridged card note the card at the bottom of the hand that is placed beneath Spectator A's hand.*)

7. Now take the cards within which Spectator B has placed his or her cards and put these cards on top of the cards within which Spectator A has placed his or her cards. The spectators may then cut and complete at will (*see the "Introduction" for an explanation of "cut and complete"*). Finally, you cut either the bridged card to the bottom of the pack or, after turning the cards face-up and spreading them to show the mix, you cut the pack to place your noted card at the bottom of the face-down pack. You then deal out from this pack eight 6-card hands, placing a card in turn on each hand, the

order of dealing in each 8-card dealing sequence being determined by the spectators.

8. You now pick up each hand in turn and, with the backs of the cards towards yourself, you fan or spread the cards and ask each spectator to say if they see their card.

9. If neither does, discard the hand. When Spectator A does, take that hand and place it face-down in front of yourself and to the left. When Spectator B does, take that hand and place it face-down in front of yourself and to the right.

10. Now place Spectator A's cards on top of Spectator B's cards. As you are picking up the cards and going through this move explain to the spectators they are now going to play a game of "SNAP".

11. Deal out face-down cards from the packet to the spectators. Deal the cards to each spectator **consecutively** beginning with Spectator A (*For an explanation of the term "consecutively" see the "Introduction".*)

12. Remind them that when they see their card they should say "SNAP!"

13. Invite Spectator B to turn his packet of cards face-up—when he or she does so Spectator A should see his or her card and say "SNAP".

14. Now invite Spectator A to turn over the top card of his packet—when he or she does so Spectator B should see his or her card and say "SNAP".

15. In the event of both spectators seeing their card in the same hand take that hand and place it face-down in front of yourself on the table. Gather up all the other hands and place them aside. Now deal out face-down onto the table the cards of the selected hand, dealing:

1	2	3
4	5	6

(This will place the spectators' cards at positions 2 and 5. A's card at position 2 and B's card at position 5.) Group the face-down cards in pairs: 1/4, 2/5, 3/6. Tell the spectators that you will "take out" a pair—which you do, either 1/4 or 3/6. Assuming that you have taken 1/4, you place this pair face-down in front of yourself on the table. You then invite one of the spectators to "take out" a pair. If the spectator chooses 3/6 take this from him or her and place it face-down in front of yourself, leaving 2/5 face-down on the table. If the spectator chooses 2/5 pick up 3/6 and place it face-down in front of yourself. In any case, the required pair 2/5 is either in the spectator's hands or on the table. If the spectator has the cards in hand instruct him or her to keep one card and give the other card to the other spectator. If the cards are on the table each takes one of the cards. Invite them now to turn the cards face-up and say "SNAP" if they see their card.

"Think Of An Ace"

Effect

A spectator is asked to think of one of the four Aces. The Aces are placed in the pack and as each Ace is placed the pack is cut by the spectator. The pack is then dealt out into four hands, one of which is chosen by the spectator. From this hand the spectator spells out the thought-of card.

Performance

1. This trick also appears as *"Just Think of An Ace"* in the routine described in the chapter *"Magic Aces"*. However, as it is ideally suited to be included in a "four-trick any-pack" block in this routine it is repeated here with some minor amendments to the handling and presentation.

2. Extract the four Aces from the pack and place them face-up on the table, overlapping each other so that only the left-hand index is displayed in the order AC (bottom), AH, AS, AD (top fully displayed). (*NOTE: A useful mnemonic is "Curly Hair Settles Down".*)

3. Shuffle the rest of the pack and cut the bridged card to the bottom of the pack. If you are not using a bridged card proceed to paragraph 11.

4. Instruct the spectator to look at the Aces and to think of and remember any one of them.

5. Collect the Aces together and turn them face-down (*NOTE: They should now be from the top AC – AH – AS – AD.*)

6. Take each Ace, separately and in turn, off the top of the face-down pile of Aces and place it in the "middle" of the pack under control of the bridge card (*for details on how this is done see the relevant section in the chapter on "Handling and Sleights-of-Hand"*). Each time an Ace is placed in the pack allow the spectator to cut and complete the pack before the bridged card is cut to the bottom of the pack (*for an explanation of the term "cut and complete" see the "Introduction"*). On the final cut of the bridged card to the bottom of the pack the Aces will be at the top of the face-down pack in order from the top AD – AS – AH – AC.

7. The spectator may now cut and complete the pack, at will. When the cutting has been completed the bridged card should be cut to the bottom of the pack.

8. Now deal out the top 13 cards of the face-down pack into a face-down pile on the table, then the next 13 cards, then another 13 cards and then place the last 13 cards face-down in a pile on the table **without dealing them out**. (*NOTE: The Aces are now at the bottom of the first pile dealt out in the order from the top of AC – AH – AS – AD and the bridged card is at the bottom of the last 13 card packet placed on the table.*)

9. You now need to organise the pack to allow for the spelling out of the spectator's thought-of Ace. Your aim is to get the pile with the bridged card at the bottom (the last pile placed on the table and which is Pile 4) on top of the first pile dealt (which has the Aces at the bottom and which is Pile 1) or, alternatively, to get Pile 4 to the bottom of the re-constituted pack with Pile 1 at the top of the pack with the other two piles (Pile 2 and Pile 3) in any order between them. This can be achieved as follows:

a. Invite the spectator to choose any two piles:
    - If the spectator chooses Pile 1 and either Pile 2 or Pile 3 place Pile 1 on the other chosen pile and the other pile on Pile 4.
    - If the spectator chooses Pile 4 and Pile 1 place Pile 4 on Pile 1 and then place Pile 2 on Pile 3 or Pile 3 on Pile 2.
    - If the spectator chooses Pile 2 and Pile 3 place either one on the other and then Pile 4 on Pile 1.

b. Allow the spectator now to choose any of the combined piles:
    - If the spectator chooses the pile that does not contain the bridged card place the pile the spectator has chosen on the top or the bottom of the other pile as directed by the spectator.
    - If the spectator chooses the pile with the bridged card at the bottom—the other pile is placed on the top or at the bottom of the pile with the bridged card at the bottom.
    - If the spectator chooses the pile **containing the bridged card and the Aces** that pile is placed on the top, or the bottom, of the other pile.

c. Cutting the bridged card to the bottom of the reconstituted pack sets the pack with Pile 1 (with the Aces) at the top of the pack.

10. It is now possible for the spectator to spell out his or her thought-of Ace from the face-down pack using the

following spelling-out procedure taking a card off the top of the pack for each letter.

a. "A – C – E – O – F – C – L – U – B – S"
The AC is at the "S" of the spelling
b. "A – C – E – O – F – H – E – A – R – T – S"
The AH is at the "S" of the spelling
c. "A – C – E – O – F – S – P – A – D – E – S"
The AS is the next card in the pack, ie. the top card of the remainder of the pack.
d. "A – C – E – O – F – D – I – A – M – O – N – D – S"
The AD is at the "S" of the spelling.

11. If you have chosen to perform the trick without the use of a bridged card proceed as follows:

a. Extract the four Aces from the pack and place them face-up on the table as described at paragraph 2 above.
b. Shuffle the rest of the pack and allow the spectator to shuffle the pack. As you take the pack back from the spectator glimpse and note the identity of the bottom card of the pack.
c. Instruct the spectator to look at the Aces and to think of and remember any one of them.
d. Collect the Aces together and turn them face down (*NOTE: They should now be from the top AC – AH – AS – AD.*)
e. Deal off from the top of the rest of the face-down pack two hands each of 12-cards. Place the remainder of the pack to one side (*NOTE: Your noted card is the bottom card of this packet.*)
f. Invite the spectator to choose any one of the two face-down hands you have just dealt. Take the hand

that has **not** been chosen and place it face-down on top of the cards you put aside at paragraph 11e above and take the hand that has been chosen and deal from it four 3-card packets: A – B – C – D from left to right.

g. Pick up the face-down Aces and place an Ace in turn from the top of the Ace packet on top of the packets A – B – C – D in that order. Then pick up the packets placing D on C, then DC on B, then DCB on A.

h. Hand the combined packet to the spectator and invite him or her to place it either on top or below the cards placed aside. He or she may then cut and complete the pack as many times as he or she wishes (*for an explanation of the term "cut and complete" see the "Introduction".*)

i. You then perform a Charlier Shuffle or mix, allowing the spectator to determine how many cards you take at each stage (*for details of how to perform this shuffle see the chapter on "Handling and Sleights-of-Hand".*) At the conclusion of the shuffle the spectator may cut and complete the pack.

j. You now take the pack, turn it face-up and spread it to show the mix of the cards. In doing so you locate the card you noted at paragraph 11b above and split the pack at this point to make this card the bottom card of the pack when the pack is turned face-down.

k. Deal out the pack into four 13-card hands, dealing to each hand **consecutively** from the top of the face-down pack (*for an explanation of the term "dealing consecutively" see the "Introduction".*) You should note that the first hand you deal to will contain the Aces at the position to conclude the trick, ie. they are the bottom cards of the face-down hand in the order AC – AH – AS – AD. You now force the spectator to choose this hand using Magician's Choice (*for an explanation of the term "Magician's Choice" see the relevant section in the chapter "Handling and Sleights-of-Hand".*)

I. To do this proceed as follows:

- First place the face-down hands in a row A – B – C – D, where A is the first hand dealt.

- Invite the spectator to "Pick out two piles— touch the piles you want to pick out."

- If the spectator chooses any two of B, C, or D take the two chosen hands and place them aside. If the spectator chooses A and any one of B, C, or D take the hands **not** chosen from B, C, and D and place them aside. In any case A and one other hand remain.

- Invite the spectator to "*Now* pick one of **those** piles."

- If the spectator chooses the pile other than A place that pile aside. If the spectator chooses Pile A place the other pile aside. In any case, pile A is left for the conclusion of the trick.

- Give the face-down hand to the spectator to spell out his or her thought-of Ace using the spelling-out procedure described at paragraph 10 above.

"A Magic Number"

EFFECT

A spectator has a free (secret) choice of a card from a hand of eight cards dealt to him or her from a shuffled pack. The spectator returns the cards, including the selected card, to the pack which is then shuffled. The performer then, using the pack, proceeds to arrive at a "magic number" which the spectator may, if he or she wishes, change by using the pack again. Once the spectator has arrived at a number he or she wishes to use the performer counts that many cards off the pack and arrives at the selected card.

PERFORMANCE

1. Allow the spectator to shuffle and cut the pack as he or she wishes. Finally, you take the pack and cut it, taking the bridged card to the bottom of the pack. If you are not using a bridged card, when you take the pack from the spectator glimpse and take note of the bottom card of the pack.
2. Now deal off from the top of the face-down pack eight face-down cards and invite the spectator, if he or she wishes, to exchange any of the cards for others from the pack.
3. Instruct the spectator to shuffle or mix the cards and to make a secret note of the top card of the face-down packet.
4. As he or she does so give the rest of the pack an over-hand shuffle, bringing the bridged card from the

bottom of the pack to the top of the pack (*for details on how to do this see the relevant section in the chapter "Handling and Sleights-of-Hand".*) Alternatively, cut and complete the pack, open the pack at the bridged card and allow this card to drop onto the top of the bottom packet before taking that packet to the top of the pack (*for a definition of the term "cut and complete" see the "Introduction".*) If you are not using a bridge card, transfer the bottom card to the top of the pack using a controlled cut (*for details of how to perform this move see the relevant section in the chapter "Handling and Sleights-of-Hand".*) Alternatively, use a modified Charlier Cut or mix to transfer the card from the bottom to the top of the pack (*for details of how to do this see the relevant section in the chapter "Handling and Sleights of Hand".*)

5. The spectator now places his or her packet of cards face-down either on the top or bottom of the face-down pack and cuts and completes the pack, at will. You take the pack and mix the cards using a Charlier Shuffle. The spectator then cuts and completes the pack, at will. Finally, you cut the bridged card to the bottom of the pack. If you are not using a bridged card in the performance of the trick after the Charlier Shuffle and the spectator's cuts you turn the pack face-up and spread it to show the mix of the cards. Note the position of the card you identified at paragraph 1 above and cut the pack to place this card and the cards below it at the bottom of the face-down pack. (*For details of how to perform the Charlier Shuffle see the relevant section in the chapter "Handling and Sleights-of-Hand".*)

6. You now explain that you are going to arrive at "a magic number" by using cards from the pack. You explain that you will do this by dealing out face-up cards from the

top of the pack in a line counting down from the top of the line from 10 to 1, ie. "10", "9", "8", "7", etc. If there is a coincidence of the value of the card with the number you will stop the line at that card and start another line. If there is no coincidence of value and number you will close that line by taking the next card in the pack and placing it face-down on the line of face-up cards. You then begin another line. You will do this until you have counted out four lines. You will then add up the values of the cards at the end of the lines that have not been closed off. This is "the magic number".

7. Demonstrate the procedure as you describe it, telling the spectator that the court cards (ie. Jacks, Queens, Kings) can be given any value—but that once this value is assigned to them then those cards retain that value throughout the dealing out.

8. After the demonstration gather up the cards that have been dealt out and allow the spectator to shuffle them. Then place them face-down on top of the face-down pack.

9. Now go through this process again, after inviting the spectator to fix the value to be used for the court cards.

10. When you have "the magic number" ask the spectator if he or she is happy with it or would he or she like to go through the procedure again to find another number. Do as the spectator wishes.

11. Once you have "the magic number" count off from the top of the face-down cards you have left in the pack to that number. The card at that number will be the card selected by the spectator.

"Real Magic"

EFFECT

From a shuffled and cut pack the spectator cuts off about half of the pack, shuffles it, and then counts the number of cards that have been cut off. The spectator now adds together the two digits of this number to arrive at a single digit number. The spectator then shuffles the cards he or she has cut off and then deals out cards from the packet equal to this number and secretly notes the card at that number. The spectator then shuffles the remaining cards in the packet, reconstitutes the packet and adds it to the shuffled remainder of the pack. The performer then proceeds to spell out a magic phrase, revealing the spectator's selected card on completion of the spelling-out.

PERFORMANCE

1. Allow the spectator to shuffle the pack and to cut and complete it, at will. (*For an explanation of the term "cut and complete" see the "Introduction".*)
2. When the spectator has completed his or her cutting, take the face-down pack and cut the bridged card to the bottom of the pack. If you are not using a bridge card proceed directly to paragraph 3 below.
3. Place the pack face-down on the table and invite the spectator to cut off about the top half of the pack, to shuffle the cards taken off, and then to count how many cards he or she has cut off by dealing them out in a

pile face-down on the table. Encourage the spectator to take a reasonable number of cards but stress that he or she may take less than half of the pack or more if he or she so wishes. (*NOTE: The trick will work for any number of cards from 10 to 49.*)

4. You should note the number of cards counted out by the spectator.

5. You now instruct the spectator to add together the two digits of the number to arrive at an "arbitrary" number. You also announce that you now intend to produce some "real magic".

6. When the "arbitrary" number has been arrived at instruct the spectator to shuffle the cards he or she has just counted and then to deal off face-down in a pile on the table the number of cards corresponding to the "arbitrary" number. When the spectator has done so instruct him or her to (secretly) note the card at that number, to shuffle the rest of the cards, and to place them face-down on top of the cards on the table. (*NOTE: This places these cards on top of the noted card.*)

7. You now hand the spectator the rest of the pack and tell him or her to shuffle it.

8. You take these cards back and, if you are using a bridged card you cut that card to the bottom after shuffling the cards yourself. If you are not using a bridged card, you shuffle the cards yourself and note the card at the bottom of the pack after the shuffle. The spectator now places the cards on the table face-down either on top or below the rest of the pack and cuts and completes, at will. Finally, you cut the bridged card to the bottom of the pack or, if you are not using a bridged card, spread the pack face-up to show the mix, and cut your noted card to place it at the bottom of the pack.

9. You can now spell out, as appropriate, from the top of the face-down pack the phrase to reveal the spectator's noted card. The spelling system is as follows:

a. **10-19 cards taken:** Spell out, taking a card for each letter, "M – A – G – I – C   C – A – R – D – S", *and take the card at the last letter of the spelling.*

b. **20-29 cards taken:** Spell out, taking a card for each letter, "N – O – W   F – O – R   S – O – M – E   R – E – A – L   M – A – G – I – C", *and take the card at the last letter of the spelling.*

c. **30-39 cards taken:** Spell out, taking a card for each letter, "N – O – W   F – O – R   S – O – M – E   R – E – A – L   M – A – G – I – C   H – E – Y   P – R – E – S – T – O", *and take the card at the last letter of the spelling.*

d. **40-49 cards taken:** Spell out, taking a card for each letter, "N – O – W   F – O – R   S – O – M – E   R – E – A – L   M – A – G – I – C   H – E – Y   P – R – E – S – T – O   A – N – D   S – H – A – Z – A – M", *and take the card at the last letter of the spelling.*

The Two-Pack Trick

"Nobody Knows Anything"

EFFECT

Both packs are thoroughly shuffled and cut. The spectator then places a selected card between blocks of cards cut off from both packs. The spectator cuts this combined packet as many times as he or she wishes. The performer takes the packet and divides it into two parts, which are shuffled by the spectator and by the performer. There then follows a series of cuts and shuffles and mixing of the cards to produce a packet of indiscriminately mixed face-up and face-down cards. When the packet is given a final shuffle all the face-down cards are seen to be a mix of the two back colours. When the face-up cards are turned over all the backs are of one back colour except for one which is of the opposite colour and which, when it is turned face-up, is revealed as the spectator's selected card.

PERFORMANCE

1. Hand the Blue pack to the spectator and allow him or her to shuffle and cut it, at will.
2. When the spectator has finished take the Blue pack, shuffle it and cut and complete. Then turn the pack face-up and spread it to show the mix of the cards. Finally, cut the face-up pack and note the identity of the card that, when you turn the pack face-down, will be the bottom card of the face-down pack. Turn the pack face-down and place it on the table. (*For an*

explanation of the term "cut and complete" see the "Introduction".)

3. Now hand the Red pack to the spectator and instruct him or her to shuffle and cut it, at will.

4. When the spectator has finished take the Red pack, shuffle it and cut and complete. Then turn the pack face-up and spread it to show the mix of the cards. In doing so, locate the position of the card you identified at paragraph 2 (ie. the card that is the bottom card of the Blue pack) and split the pack at this point in such a way that that card will be the top card of the Red pack when that pack is turned face-down. Turn the pack face-down and place it on the table.

5. Invite the spectator to take whichever pack he or she wishes and to place it face-down in front of him- or herself.

6. If the spectator has taken the Blue pack (the pack with your noted card as its bottom card) instruct him or her to cut off about $1/_3$ of the cards from the top of the pack and to place them face-down on the table. You then invite the spectator to take any card he or she wishes from **within** the Red pack, to note it secretly, and to place it face down on top of the cards he or she has just cut off the other pack. Having done this, the spectator cuts off about $1/_3$ of the cards from what is left of the other pack (the Blue pack) and places these cards on top of the selected card. He or she then cuts off about $1/_3$ of the cards from the top of the Red pack and places these cards on top of the packet containing the selected card. He or she may now cut and complete the cards, at will.

7. If the spectator takes the Red pack (the pack with your noted card as the top card) instruct him or her to take out any card from **within** that pack, note it secretly, and

to place it face-down on the table. The spectator then cuts off about 1/3 of the cards from the other pack (the Blue pack), places them face-down on the table, and places the selected card face-down on top of them. The spectator now cuts off about $\frac{1}{3}$ of what is left of the Blue pack and places these cards on top of the selected card. He or she then cuts off about $\frac{1}{3}$ of the Red pack and places these cards on top of the packet containing the selected card. The spectator may now cut and complete the cards, at will.

8. Having put aside the cards from both packs not used in either paragraph 6 or paragraph 7 above, you take the mixed card packet and cut it a few more times.

9. You then turn the packet face-up and spread it to show the mix of the cards. In doing so you note the location of the card you identified at paragraphs 2 and 4 above and cut the packet so that when the packet is face-down this card will be the top card of the packet. Having done this you place the packet face-down on the table.

10. You now cut the packet at about half-way down. Turn the cards that you have cut off face-up and hand them to the spectator. Instruct the spectator to shuffle the cards.

11. Turn the cards left on the table face-up and shuffle them yourself.

12. Now cut-off about half of the cards you have, turn them over, and hand them to the spectator. Instruct the spectator to cut off about half of the cards he or she has, to turn them over, and hand them to you. You both then shuffle the cards you have been given into the cards you have left. Repeat this procedure TWO more times.

13. When this has been done instruct the spectator to place his or her cards on the table. **Turn over the cards you**

have and place them on top of the spectator's cards. The spectator may then cut and complete at will.

14. Take the packet from the table, **turn it over**, cut it into roughly equal parts and then shuffle the two parts together. Now spread out the cards to show the mix of face-up cards and Blue and Red face-down cards in the packet. Point out that nobody could now know which cards are face-up and which cards are face-down.

15. Then deal out the pack, dealing the face-up cards into one pile and the face-down cards into a second pile. The face-down pack should contain face-down cards of both back colours. Point this out and then turn over the face-up pile and spread it out. All the face-down cards will be of one colour—except for one card which will be of the other colour. Turn this card over to reveal the card selected by the spectator at paragraph 6-7 above.

(*NOTE: You should ensure at paragraph 12 that the spectator **does not turn over** the cards into which he or she is shuffling the cards you have passed to him or her.*)

The Final Tricks

"Same Number—Same Card"
(For One Spectator)

EFFECT

The picture or court cards are taken out of the pack. A spectator is asked to choose any one of them. It is placed face-up on the table and the spectator assigns to it any value from 1-10. The pack is then cut by the spectator and from the pack is then extracted a sequence of cards using the value given by the spectator to the court card as the start of the sequence. The total value of the extracted cards and the value given to the court card is determined and a note is taken of this total and of the identity of the final card arrived at. The process is then repeated two more times. In every case the spectator allocates a different value to the court card. However, in every case the total arrived at and the final card of the sequence will be the same.

PERFORMANCE

1. In the routine this trick will normally follow the trick *"Nobody Knows Anything"*. However, if you have chosen not to perform this trick it will follow either *"Divination"* or *"Real Magic"*. Depending upon which trick it follows proceed as described below:

    a. If the trick follows *"Nobody Knows Anything"* you will have on the table a mixture of two packs, some cards face-up and some cards face-down. Instruct the spectator to collect one of the packs, to order it face-down, and to replace it in its carton. You collect the other pack. As you do so ensure that you have from 10 to Ace in the bottom half of the pack. When the spectator has finished with the other pack, hand the top half of your pack to him or her to extract the court cards from it. You do likewise with your half. As you do so, order the bottom cards of your face-down half from 10 to Ace in that order. Then take the **non-court** *cards* from the spectator and place them face-down on top of your face-down packet.

b. If the trick follows on from *"Divination"* you already have the basis of the order of cards you require at the bottom of the face-down pack in the cards you are holding. In fact, you will have two sequences of cards that could be used as the basis. If the sequences have one or more court cards in them extract these cards and place them aside. As you do so, order one of the sequences from 10 to Ace and randomly disturb the order of the other sequence. With the packet face-down place the 10 to Ace sequence at the bottom of the packet (the suits are immaterial). You may, of course, have two sequences of 10 to Ace in your hand. In which case you merely order one of them appropriately and randomly disturb the order of the other sequence. Finally, if you find that you require cards to complete a sequence of 10 to Ace then the necessary cards are in the discard pile from the trick *"Divination"*. In this case, instruct the spectator to gather up the discard pile, to extract the court cards from it and place them aside, and to hand you the other cards, which you can then use to complete your sequence. In all cases, you instruct the spectator to shuffle the cards he or she has and to hand them to you. Again, in all cases, you will finish with a face-down pack with the bottom ten cards in the sequence 10 to Ace in that order.

c. If the trick follows *"Real Magic"* hand about half of the cards to the spectator, who should extract the court cards, place them aside, and shuffle the remaining cards. Meanwhile, you extract the court cards from your half of the pack, place them aside, and, in doing so, as far as you are able, create a 10 to Ace sequence in the other cards. In discarding the court cards place them in a random face-up / face-down order. Take the shuffled cards from the spectator and hand him or her the face-up / face-down cards. Instruct the spectator to go through them to ensure that there are no non-court cards among them. This should provide sufficient distraction to allow you to complete your 10 to Ace sequence and place it at the bottom of the face-down pack.

2. By whatever means you have achieved it, you now have a face-down pack (less the court cards) with the bottom ten cards ordered from 10 to Ace. Instruct the spectator to choose any one of the court cards, to place the chosen card face-up on the table, and to assign to it any value from 1 to 10. He or she should make a note of or remember this number.

3. You now invite the spectator to cut and complete the face-down pack. (*For an explanation of the term "cut and complete" see the "Introduction".*)

4. You then take the pack and count off from the top of it a number of cards equal to the value the spectator has

assigned to the court card. As the cards are counted their order is not reversed, ie. each card is counted off beneath the preceding card. The packet that is counted off is turned face-up to reveal the face card of the packet and the packet is then placed face-up on the court card so that only the left hand index of the court card can be seen. You then use the value of the face card of the packet as the number of cards you next count off the top of the pack. This packet is placed on the preceding packet as described above and the process is continued through the pack, until you reach the final card of the pack or until there are insufficient cards left in the pack to match the value of the face-card of the packet.

5. The values of all the revealed cards and the value assigned to the initial face-up card are now added together.

6. The spectator is instructed to note and remember this number and to note and remember the identity of the revealed card.

7. Having arrived at the total, you collect up all the cards from left to right, sliding each card or packet beneath the subsequent card or packet, and then place the pack face-down on the table, or the cards you have collected up face-down on the face-down cards you have left over from the counting-out.

8. Now repeat the process described in paragraphs 4-6 above, having forecast that you will arrive at the same total and the same final card, and having allowed the spectator to assign a different number from 1 to 10 to the court card, which you take from the top of the pack and place face-up on the table. You will arrive at the same total and at the same final card.

9. Collect up the cards as before, place the court card face-up on the table, and instruct the spectator to assign yet another value from 1 to 10 to it. Then go through the counting-out procedure again and once again arrive at the same total and the same final card.

"Everybody Shouts"
(For Two Or More Spectators)

EFFECT
(USING A BRIDGED CARD)

A number of spectators in turn are handed the pack and told to shuffle it. The performer then takes the pack and asks the first spectator to take the top card of the pack, secretly note it, and then shuffle it back into the pack. This procedure is repeated for any number of spectators. When all the spectators have taken and noted a card the performer deals out the same number of cards as there are spectators who have taken a card. The spectators look at these cards and confirm that their cards are there. The performer takes the cards and places them face-up on the table in a row. The performer then asks the spectators at a given signal to shout out the name of their card and to pick the card up from the table. They all shout out and attempt to pick up the same card at the given signal.

EFFECT
(NOT USING A BRIDGED CARD)

The trick begins and ends as described above for the bridged card, the difference being the series of cuts and deals leading to the selection of the spectators' cards.

Performance
(Using a bridged card)

1. Each spectator involved is handed the pack in turn and instructed to shuffle it.

2. You take the pack back, shuffle it, and cut at the bridged card, allowing the bridged card to fall on top of the packet that will be the top of the whole pack when you complete the cut and the cards are turned face-down.

3. You invite one of the spectators to take the top card of the face-down pack, note it secretly without revealing it either to you or to any other spectator, and then to shuffle it back into the pack.

4. You take the pack back, shuffle it, and then cut the bridged card to the bottom of the pack. The next spectator is then invited to take the bottom card, note it secretly without revealing it either to you or any other spectator, and then to shuffle it back into the pack.

5. You repeat paragraphs 2 and 3 and paragraphs 2 and 4 alternately until all the spectators involved have taken and selected a card.

6. Once the final spectator has noted a card and shuffled it back into the pack, you take the pack back, shuffle it and cut at the bridged card, allowing the bridged card to fall on top of the packet that will be the top of the whole pack when you complete the cut and the pack is face-down.

7. Now deal out, face-down onto the table as many cards as there are spectators who have taken and noted a card. Having done so, pick up the cards and mix them. With the cards still face-down hand the packet to each spectator in turn and ask them to confirm that their card is in the packet.

8. You now take the packet and spread it out face-up on the table. You instruct the spectators on your count of "1–2–3" to shout out the name of their card and pick it up. They will all shout out and attempt to pick up the same card (the bridged card).

Performance
(Not using a bridged card)

1. Each spectator involved is handed the pack and instructed to shuffle it.
2. You take the pack back, shuffle it, place it face-down on the table and instruct the first spectator to take the top card. Instruct him or her to note it secretly without revealing it either to you or to any of the other spectators. When he or she has done so ask him or her to place the card face-down on top of the face-down pack.
3. A second spectator is instructed to cut off about half of the pack, which he or she should place face-down on the table. Now instruct the spectator to take the bottom part of the pack, turn it face-up, and place it on top of the packet he or she has just cut off. Finally, you instruct him or her to turn over the whole pack.
4. You now take the pack, without turning it over or disturbing it in any way, and cut it in exactly the same way as the spectator, including the final turning over of the pack. When you make your initial cut off the top of the pack you should ensure that you are cutting **below** the level at which the spectator cut. (*For a full description and explanation of this handling see the relevant section in the chapter "Handling and Sleights-of-Hand".*)
5. When you have completed the whole procedure you place the pack in front of the second spectator and instruct him or her to take the first face-down card

in the pack. He or she should note the card secretly without revealing it to either you or another spectator.

6. When the spectator has done this instruct him or her to place the card face-down on the table, to turn any face-up cards in the pack face-down, and to place the face-down pack on top of it.

7. You take the face-down pack, cut off about the top ¾ of the cards, turn these cards over and place them at the bottom of the pack. You then turn the pack over, cut off about the top ½ of the cards, turn these cards over and place them at the bottom of the pack. You turn the pack over and spread it until you sight the first face-up card. You cut the pack at this point leaving the face-down card above the face-up card in place. The other face-down cards above that card you turn and place at the bottom of the pack. You now place the pack on the table and instruct the third spectator to take the top card of the pack and to note it secretly without revealing it to either you or another spectator.

8. When the spectator has done this instruct him or her to place the card on top of the face-down pack. Immediately, turn to the fourth spectator and ask him or her how many cards between 10 and 20 he or she wants you to deal off the pack. Deal off face-down onto the table the required number of cards into a pile, and instruct the spectator to cut off from the top of this pile as many cards as he or she wishes, and immediately either put them in a pocket or hide them. Point out that this is because you do not want to know how many cards have been cut and you do not want the spectator to know now many cards he or she has cut off. When the spectator has made the cut and hidden the cards ask how many cards he or she would now like you to deal off the pack. Deal off face-down

onto the face-down cards left on the table the required number of cards and instruct the spectator to repeat the procedure of cutting off a number of cards from the pile and hiding them with the cards already cut off. You now pick up the cards left in the pile on the table and, without disturbing their order, place them on top of the pack. You then immediately deal out into a face-down pile on the table a number of cards that is the total of the cards dealt in the two previous deals. You do this without counting them out aloud or stating the number.

9. You now instruct the spectator to take all the cards he or she has cut off and to count them. You tell him or her that you will use this number to determine how many cards are cut off the packet you have just dealt out. While the spectator is counting the cut-off cards pick up the pile you have dealt onto the table and place it on the top of the pack. When the spectator has completed the count take his or her cards and place them at the bottom of the pack. You then count off a number of cards from the top of the pack corresponding to the number he or she counted. These cards are transferred to the bottom of the pack. The spectator is instructed to take the top card of the pack. He or she should note it secretly without revealing it to either you or any other spectator.

10. When the spectator has done this instruct him or her to place the card face-down on top of the face-down pack. If more spectators are to be involved in the trick you should go through the sequence of procedures described in paragraphs 3-9 above again to the point at which all the spectators have taken out and noted a card. *The final spectator to take a card should replace it on **the top** of the face-down pack.*

11. In taking the pack back note the identity of the bottom card of the pack. Having done so, allow each of the spectators who are taking part in the trick to cut and complete (*for an explanation of the term "cut and complete" see the "Introduction"*.) You then take the pack, turn it face-up and spread the cards to show the mix of the cards. Note the location of your noted card and cut the pack to place this card at the bottom of the face-down pack.

12. Once this has been done you should proceed as described at paragraphs 7 and 8 above, for the performance using a bridged card.

"OUT OF THE BOX"

Opening The Pack

S TART WITH THE SEALED carton of cards on the table. Invite a spectator to remove the wrapping, break the seal, and to take the pack out of the carton. Take the pack from the spectator and remove the Joker cards and any other extraneous cards. In doing so do not disturb the order of the pack.

The sequence of the cards in the "*Bicycle Rider Back*" pack is (when the pack is face-down): Ace to King (Hearts)—Ace to King (Clubs)—King to Ace (Diamonds)—King to Ace (Spades).

Mixing The Pack

If you do not intend to use a bridge card or sleights-of-hand in the performance of the routine proceed directly to the next section of this chapter. If you are using a bridged card and wish to give the impression to the spectator that you are mixing the pack proceed as described in the next paragraph.

With the **Ace of Spades** as the bridged card you may allow the spectator or any number of spectators to cut and complete the pack, provided that, finally, you cut the bridged card to the bottom of the pack. Additionally, using the bridged card you may perform a false mix of the pack. (*For details of how to produce the bridged card and how to use the bridged card see the relevant section in the chapter "Handling and Sleights of Hand" and for an explanation of the term "cut and complete" see the "Introduction".*)

Arranging The Pack

If you wish to arrange the pack without using a bridged card begin by stating that it would be as well to make sure that all the 52 cards are there in the pack. Count out the first 13 cards from the top of the face-down pack and place them on the table. Do this without reversing their order, ie, as you count the cards off the pack each card is placed beneath the one or ones already counted. Continue counting off the next 13 cards (again without reversing their order) and place these cards on top of the cards already on the table. Continue counting out the rest of the pack (still not reversing the order of the cards) and when the count is completed pick up the cards from the table and place them on top of the cards in hand.

The sequence of the cards is now: Ace to King (Clubs)— Ace to King (Hearts)—King to Ace (Diamonds)—King to Ace (Spades).

To rearrange the sequence of the cards using the bridged card (**Ace of Spades**) begin by asking a spectator whether he or she would like to have the top half of the pack or the bottom half. Irrespective of the reply count out the first 26 cards from the top of the face-down pack and place them on the table. Do this without reversing their order as described in the preceding paragraph. You then place the remainder of the pack (without counting them out) by the side of the cards already on the table. Finally, you instruct the spectator to take the part of the pack that he or she chose and to place it either at the top or at the bottom of the other half of the pack. The spectator may then cut and complete the pack as many times as wished, provided that, finally, you cut the bridged card to the bottom of the pack. The sequence of the cards is then as stated above.

Setting The Pack

State that in order to make sure that the pack is thoroughly mixed you are going to deal it out into four piles.

Deal out the cards from the top of the pack face-down into four piles, placing a card in turn on each pile to give:

Pile 1 – Pile 2 – Pile 3 – Pile 4.

Reconstitute the pack by placing Pile 4 on Pile 3 and then those cards on Pile 2, and then all those cards on Pile 1.

Repeat the procedure described in the two preceding paragraphs one more time.

Alternative Packs

The mixing, arranging, and setting of the pack described in the first three sections of this chapter assume that the cards used are a "*Bicycle Rider Back*" pack. With this pack when the cards are removed from the sealed carton and the Joker and extraneous cards are removed the order of the cards from the top in the face-down pack is Ace to King (Hearts), Ace to King (Clubs), King to Ace (Diamonds), and King to Ace (Spades). The W.H. Smith *"Standard"* pack has exactly the same arrangement and the handling required for the mixing, arrangement, and setting of this pack is therefore as described in the first three sections of this chapter.

The Waddington *"No 1"* pack has a different order in that all the suits in the sequence Hearts, Clubs, Diamonds, Spades are arranged King to Ace. It therefore requires different handling to put the cards into the necessary pre-arrangement for the routine. To do this proceed as follows:

a. *Mixing The Pack.* If you are not using a bridged card proceed directly to the next paragraph: *"Arranging the Pack"*. If you are using a bridged card proceed as described in the section *"Mixing The Pack"* in this chapter.

b. *Arranging The Pack.* To re-arrange the pack to the sequence required for the routine proceed as follows:

> State that you need to confirm that all 52 cards are in the pack.

> Deal off from the top of the pack face-down onto the table the first 26 cards, counting them aloud as you do so. In doing this you are reversing the order of the cards.

> Continue the count from "27-52" with the cards in hand. In performing the count do **not** reverse

the order of the cards, ie, as you count the cards each card is placed **beneath** the one or ones already counted.

When the count is completed place the cards from the table on top of the cards in hand.

The sequence of the pack is now: Ace to King (Clubs), Ace to King (Hearts), King to Ace (Diamonds), King to Ace (Spades), which is the sequence required to perform the routine.

c. *Setting The Pack*. The pack is set as described in the section "*Setting The Pack*".

The Routine

First Trick:
"Cards And Numbers"

Effect

Two piles of face-down cards are dealt out from the pack. The spectator selects any number from 1 to 26. This having been done the performer moves a card forward from his or her packet and invites the spectator to move forward from his or her packet the card at the number selected. When the cards are revealed they are of the same value and colour. The performer then moves another card forward from his or her packet and invites the spectator to cut a number of cards from his or her packet and to use them to arrive at an arbitrary number. When her or she goes to the card in his or her packet corresponding to that number they find that again it is of the same value and colour as the performer's card.

Performance

1. If you are not using a bridged card proceed directly to paragraph 3.
2. If you are performing the routine using a bridged card (**Ace of Spades**) you should note that this card is now at the bottom of the pack and you may, therefore, if you wish, allow the spectator to cut and complete the pack, provided that, finally, you cut the bridged card to the bottom of the pack.
3. Begin by dealing out from the top of the face-down pack two piles of face-down cards—one for the spectator and one for yourself. Deal the first card to the spectator and

the second card to yourself and continue to deal, placing a card in turn on each pile until the pack is exhausted.

4. Now ask the spectator to select any number from 1 to 26.

5. Once the spectator has selected the number go through your cards (without revealing that you are counting them) to the card represented by the calculation 26 minus the spectator's number plus 1 (or, more conveniently, 27 minus the spectator's selected number). Move this card forward from the rest of the cards so that it projects from the packet for about half its length, but do not disturb its order within the packet. Then place the packet (still face-down) on the table.

6. Instruct the spectator to do exactly the same, moving forward the card at his or her stated number.

7. When the two piles of cards are turned face-up the projecting cards will be of the same value and colour.

8. Push the projecting cards back into their positions in the separate packets, turn both packets face-down, and place your cards on top of the spectator's cards.

9. Again deal out face-down two piles of cards—one for the spectator and one for yourself. Again deal the first card to the spectator and the second card to yourself and continue to deal placing a card in turn on each of the piles until each pile contains 26 cards.

10. State that in order to convince the spectator that the cards are neither marked nor arranged in some way you will choose your card first and then allow the spectator to arrive at a completely arbitrary number for the choice of his or her card.

11. In your own packet of cards go through to the 17th card from the top (again without revealing that your are counting) and display it face-down as described in paragraph 5 above.

12. If you are not using the bridged card proceed directly to paragraph 13. If you are using the bridged card (**Ace of Spades**) you should note that this card is now the bottom card of the spectator's pile of cards and you may therefore, if you wish, allow the spectator to cut and complete that pile of cards, provided that, finally, you cut the bridged card to the bottom of the pile.

13. Now allow the spectator to arrive at "a completely arbitrary" number by cutting his or her pile of cards roughly in half. You take the bottom half of the cut and place it on top of your own pile of cards in line with the non-projecting cards. You then invite the spectator to deal off face-down onto the table into a pile the cards he or she has cut off. In doing so he or she should count out the number of cards being dealt. When the dealing and the counting have been completed the spectator should add together the two digits of the number arrived at to produce a single figure "arbitrary" number, (eg, 12 = 1 + 2 = 3).

    (*Note: If on the count the spectator has cut off less than 10 cards instruct him or her to **deal** off onto the pile 10 cards from the top of the pack. Take the total then arrived at and proceed with the calculation using this total. For example, if the spectator has counted out seven cards he or she then **deals** 10 cards to make a total of 17. The calculation is then 17 = 1 + 7 = 8.*)

14. Instruct the spectator to take the cards he or she has dealt out onto the table and to deal them out from the top of the face-down packet face-down into a pile. When he or she reaches the card indicated by the number calculated at paragraph 13 above he or she should take that card and place it (still face-down) projecting about half-way forward on the other cards. The spectator should then continue dealing out the

other cards of the packet aligning them with the non-projecting cards.

15. When the two piles (the spectators and your own) are turned face-up the two projecting cards will be of the same value and the same colour.

16. Push the two projecting cards back into the separate packets, turn both packets face-down, and place the spectator's cards on top of your packet.

Second Trick:
"Bluff—Double Bluff"

EFFECT

Half the pack is taken by the spectator and the other half by the performer. The spectator now begins to deal out face-down onto the table two piles and the performer matches the dealing by simultaneously dealing out two face-down piles. At any time in the dealing the spectator may call "Bluff"—in which case he or she turns face-up one of the cards he or she has just dealt and any one of the cards just dealt by the performer. The cards match in value. Alternatively, the spectator may at any time call "Double Bluff"—in which case he or she again turns face-up one of the cards he or she has just dealt and the last two cards dealt by the performer. All the cards match in value.

PERFORMANCE

1. If you are not using a bridged card in the performance of the routine proceed directly to paragraph 3.
2. If you are using the bridged card (**Ace of Spades**) you should note that this card is now the 26th card down in the face-down pack. Tell the spectator that for the next trick you need to divide the pack between the two of you and that usually you are able to cut the pack exactly in half. Cut at the bridged card and count out the cards face-down into a pile in front of the spectator (thus reversing their order). You may, if you wish, appear slightly surprised that you have managed

to cut the pack exactly in half. Alternatively, you could have cut slightly above the bridged card in which case you would then count off the additional cards from the other packet to bring the total in the pile to 26. In any case you do not disturb the order of the bottom 26 cards of the pack, which you take as your own packet. Now proceed to paragraph 4.

3.   If you are not using a bridged card count off the top 26 cards of the face-down pack face-down into a pile in front of the spectator (thus reversing their order) and retain the bottom half of the pack for yourself (thus not reversing their order).

4.   Now instruct the spectator to deal out his or her cards side by side on the table forming two face-down piles— Pile 1 and Pile 2 (ie, he or she deals a card to Pile 1 first and then the second card to Pile 2 and so on throughout the dealing). You match the dealing with your own cards, producing Pile 3 and Pile 4. At any point in the dealing as the spectator places a card on Pile 1 he or she may call "Bluff", in which case the spectator places that card face-up on Pile 1 and the next card face-down on Pile 2. You then place your two cards face-down on your piles and invite the spectator to turn any one of them face-up. When he or she does so the card will match in value the spectator's face-up card. The spectator may also at any point in the dealing as he or she is placing a card on Pile 1 call "Double Bluff", in which case he or she places that card face-down on Pile 1 and the next card face-up on Pile 2. You then place your next two cards face-down on the appropriate piles. When the spectator turns your two cards face-up they will both match in value the spectator's face-up card.

Third Trick:
"Separating The Cards"

Effect

After the pack has been shuffled the cards are dealt out into two piles turning one card face-up and one card face-down and placing them in such a way that each pile has face-up and face-down cards. When all the cards have been dealt and when all the cards are turned face-up it is revealed that all the red cards are in one pile and all the black cards are in the other pile.

Performance

1. You now have on the table four piles of cards (Pile 1 – Pile 2 – Pile 3 – Pile 4) with face-up and face-down cards in each pile.
2. There are three possible finishes to the routine. The finish described here gives a separation of the cards by colour after the cards have been shuffled. The second (the separation of the cards by colour with the cards in numerical order) and the third (the separation of the cards by suit in numerical order) are described in a later section in this chapter.
3. If you wish to conclude the routine with the separation of the cards by colour after they have been shuffled proceed as described below.
4. Pick up each pile of cards separately and turn the face-up cards face-down. This is done by dealing from the top of the packet onto the table, turning the face-up

cards face-down as you come to them. (This reverses the order of the cards in the packet.)

5. When you have done this for all the piles place Pile 4 on Pile 3, all those cards on Pile 2, and then all those cards on Pile 1.

6. You may now allow the spectator to cut and complete the face-down pack as many times as he or she wishes. (*For an explanation of the term "cut and complete" see the "Introduction".*)

7. When the spectator has finished his or her cutting take the pack and perform a Charlier Shuffle (*For a description of how to perform this shuffle see the relevant section of the chapter "Handling and Sleights-of-Hand".*) When you have done this turn the pack face-up and invite the spectator to cut again, placing the packet he or she has cut off by the side of the other packet. If the two packets have face-cards of the same colour re-constitute the pack and invite the spectator to cut again. Continue with this procedure until a cut of the pack produces two packets with different coloured face-cards.

8. Take the two parts of the pack, turn them face-down and riffle shuffle them together or, if he or she is able to perform it, you may allow the spectator to perform the riffle shuffle. (*For a description of this shuffle see the relevant section of the chapter "Handling and Sleights-of-Hand".*)

9. Now take the face-down pack and deal it out into two piles on the table in the following way:

   a. Take the first card and place it face-up on the table.
   b. Take the next card and place it face-down on the table by the side of the first card.

c. Take the third card, turn it face-up and, if it is the same colour as the first card, place it on the same pile face-up and place the next card (the fourth card) face-down on the second pile. If the third is a different colour to the first card place it face-up on the second card and place the fourth card face-down on the first pile.

d. Continue with this process until you have two piles of cards on the table in which all the face-up cards in one pile are of one colour and all the face-up cards in the other pile are of a different colour.

10. Pick up each pile in turn and deal it out, turning all the face-down cards face-up as you come to them. They will all be of the same colour as the face-up cards.

(*NOTE: If so wished, it is possible to repeat the finish by placing any one of the piles produced on the other and then dealing out the cards as described in the section "Setting The Cards" in this chapter. When you have done this, deal out the cards into two piles, place any one on the other, and then proceed as described at paragraphs 9 and 10 above.*)

Adaptations

In performing the final trick of the routine "*Separating The Cards*" there are three possible outcomes. The recommended finish of separating the cards by colour after a riffle shuffle is as described at paragraphs 4-10 of the description of the trick "*Separating The Cards*" earlier in this chapter. It brings the routine to a satisfactorily strong conclusion. However, it does destroy the sequence of the cards. Therefore, if you wish to extend the routine using one or two tricks described in the next section of this chapter, ie "*All In Order*" and "*Same Number—Same Card*", it would be better to bring the trick to a conclusion using one of the other two finishes which are described below. They are:

a. Separating the cards by colour with the cards in a numerical order
b. Separating the cards by suit with the cards in numerical order within the suits.

The descriptions of these finishes continue from the point at which you have brought the second trick of the routine "*Bluff—Double Bluff*" to a conclusion and you now have on the table four piles of cards (1 – 2 – 3 – 4) with face-up and face-down cards in each pile.

Colour And Numerical Order

1. Pick up each pile of cards separately and turn the face-up cards face-down. As the cards must not be reversed within the piles proceed as follows: without turning the pile over take the cards in turn from the bottom of the pile, placing each card in turn on top of the preceding card and turning the face-up cards face-down as you come to them.

2. Having gone through each pile in this way place Pile 4 on Pile 3, and then those cards on Pile 2, and then all those cards on Pile 1.

3. If you are not using a bridged card proceed directly to paragraph 4 below. If you are using a bridged card you may, if you wish, introduce a false mix of the pack at this point. In any case, you should now invite the spectator to cut and complete the pack. You should then cut the pack to place the bridged card (**Ace of Spades**) to the bottom of the face-down pack. (*For a definition of the term "cut and complete" see the "Introduction" and for details on how to perform a false mix of the pack see the relevant section of the chapter "Handling and Sleights-of-Hand".*)

4. Now deal out face-down 13 cards to the spectator and instruct him or her to deal the cards out into two face-down piles. As he or she does so note to which pile he or she deals first.

5. When the deal is complete you then deal out from the pack the next 13 cards, dealing a card to each pile in turn, beginning your deal onto the pile to which the

spectator dealt second (which is the pile to which he or she did **not** deal his or her last card).

6. Having completed your deal you now deal the next 13 cards to the spectator and instruct him or her to deal the cards out in turn onto the two piles, ensuring that he or she deals first to the pile to which you were dealing second (which is the pile to which you did **not** deal your last card).

7. You now complete the procedure by dealing out the last 13 cards onto the piles, again beginning your deal onto the pile to which the spectator dealt second.

8. Having done so, invite the spectator to take away one of the piles, to turn it face-up, and to deal the cards out onto the table. You take the other pile and, keeping it face-down, deal out from the top of the pile cards face-up onto the table. One pile will be configured: "A"–"7" (Hearts), "8"–"K" (Diamonds), "A"–"7" (Diamonds), "8"–"K" (Hearts). The other will be configured in the same way in the sequence Spades, Clubs, Clubs, Spades.

Suits In Numerical Order

1. Pick up each pile of cards separately and turn the face-up cards face-down. This is done by dealing from the top of the pile onto the table, turning the face-up cards face-down as you come to them. (This reverses the order of the cards in the piles.) If you are not using a bridged card proceed directly to paragraph 3.

2. With your left hand pick up Pile 1 (which has the bridged card (**Ace of Spades**) as its top card). At the same time pick up Pile 4 with your right hand and place Pile 1 on Pile 4. Then with your left hand place either Pile 3 on Pile 2 or Pile 2 on Pile 3 as directed by the spectator. Finally, allow the spectator to determine whether Pile 1/4 is placed on top or beneath Pile 2/3 or 3/2. (*NOTE: Taking account of the configuration of the pack produced by the spectator's decision it is possible to perform a false mix of the pack except that instead of cutting the bridged card to the bottom of the pack you should allow it to drop onto the bottom portion of the pack. You then place the bottom portion on the top of the pack—thus placing the bridged card at the top of the pack.*) Proceed now directly to paragraph 4.

3. You should at this point create the impression that the cards are being indiscriminately mixed using a version of what is known as "Magician's Choice". (*For an explanation of this term see the relevant section of the chapter "Handling and Sleights-of-Hand.*") The outcome you want to achieve is to place Pile 4 and Pile 1 together in any order (ie, 4 on 1, or 1 on 4), and Pile 3 and 2 together, again in any order. The two packets can

then be placed together in any order (ie, 3–2–4–1, or 2–3–4–1, or 1–4–3–2, or 4–1–2–3). To do this proceed as follows: invite the spectator to choose any two of the four piles and to hand one to you. The spectator then places his or her pile face-down in front of him- or herself and you do the same with your pile in front of yourself. You then invite the spectator to choose any one of the other two piles and to hand the pile he or she has not selected to you. These piles are then placed by the sides of the previous piles. Having noted the positioning of the piles you now invite the spectator to select any one of his or her piles and to place it on any other pile. Depending upon his or her selection it is then possible to ensure that the required combination is produced as follows:

a. If the spectator places Pile 1 on 4, or Pile 4 on 1, or Pile 2 on 3, or Pile 3 on 2, he or she may combine the other two piles in any order and place the combined pair on the top of or at the bottom of the other pair.

b. If the spectator chooses any two piles which results in Pile 2 or 3 being combined with either Pile 1 or 4 then, having noted the order of the combination, the performer should place the other two piles appropriately at the top and/or bottom of the spectator's combined pile

4. Now deal out the top 13 cards of the pack face-down onto the table into two piles, dealing a card to each pile in turn, beginning by dealing the first card to the left.

5. Then deal out the next 13 cards into a face-down pile in front of the spectator and instruct him or her to take the pile and to deal the cards out onto the two piles you

have created. Ensure that the spectator deals the first card to the left, ie onto the right-hand pile from your point of view.

6. When the spectator's deal has been completed you deal the next 13 cards in turn onto the two piles on the table, again dealing first to your left onto the left-hand pile.

7. You now complete the procedure by dealing out the final 13 cards into a face-down pile in front of the spectator and instruct him or her to repeat the dealing at paragraph 5 above, again ensuring he or she deals first to the left, ie onto the right-hand pile from your point of view.

8. Having done so, invite the spectator to take any one of the piles, to turn it face-up, and to deal the cards out onto the table. You take the other pile and, turning it face-up, deal out from the top of the pile cards face-up onto the table. The spectator will deal out all cards by suit and in numerical order. You will deal out the other cards in an identical configuration.

Additional Tricks

The routine as described lasts for approximately 15 minutes. However, on some occasions, the performer may wish to extend it and, for this reason, four additional tricks are described in this section.

The tricks are designed to build on the routine, taking advantage of the fact that if either of the two finishes for the routine given in the section on adaptations earlier in this chapter are performed the cards will be in a known order or configuration. Additionally, two of the tricks ("*All In Order*" and "*You Can Find It*") can be performed as stand-alone tricks.

"All In Order"

Effect

The pack is separated out into the four suits which are placed face-up on the table. Each suit is shuffled to mix the order of the cards. The spectator is then invited to select any one of the suits. This having been done that pile is turned face-down and one of the other piles, selected by the spectator, is placed on it. There now follows a series of shuffles resulting in a pack of face-up and face-down cards indiscriminately mixed. The performer then extracts the face-down cards in turn from the pack and proceeds to deal them out face-up—they are the cards of the selected suit in numerical order.

Performance

1. This trick can be performed straight from the sealed carton or following on from any trick which has resulted in the cards being separated and placed in numerical order. In the latter case the numerical order can be either Ace to King or King to Ace for each suit, ie Clubs and Diamonds could be Ace to King, and Spades and Hearts could be King to Ace, or Clubs could be Ace to King, and all the other suits King to Ace. If the trick is performed straight from the sealed carton the order of cards within the suits will be for the *"Bicycle Rider Pack"* and W.H. Smith *"Standard"* packs Hearts and Clubs: Ace to King, and Diamonds and Spades: King to Ace; and for the Waddington *"No 1"* pack King to

Ace for all the suits. A third possibility is to perform the trick as a stand-alone trick at any convenient time in a routine, in which case the suits would be openly separated and arranged.

2. Begin with the four suits in separate face-up piles on the table. Each will have either an Ace or a King as its top face-up card. Invite the spectator to select any one of the suits. When he or she has done so turn all the piles face-down.

3. Now take each pile in turn and perform a Charlier Shuffle. With each pile, when you have completed the shuffle, turn over the pile and place it face-up on the table. (*For an explanation of how to perform the Charlier Shuffle see the relevant section of the chapter "Handling and Sleights-of-Hand".*) Having done this, ask the spectator to confirm his or her selected suit. Once the selection has been confirmed take whichever pile is the selected pile and turn it face-down. In doing so make a mental note of the top face-up card of the pile.

4. Next ask the spectator to select any one of the other three piles. Once this is done, take the chosen pile and place it face-up on top of the face-down pile. Then take the other two face-up piles and riffle shuffle them (face-up) into each other. Having done this, riffle shuffle this face-up packet into the packet containing the selected cards. (*NOTE: This packet of cards will have the 13 face-up cards as the top cards of the packet and 13 face-down cards as the bottom cards of the packet.*)

5. You now have the pack with the 13 cards of the selected suit spread throughout approximately the bottom half of the otherwise face-up pack. You then cut the pack taking off **a little less** than the top half of the pack and riffle shuffle the two halves of the pack together. (This, of course, will spread the cards of the selected suit

throughout the whole of the pack. However, because of the Charlier Shuffle at paragraph 3 above they will not be in numerical order.)

6. To bring the trick to its conclusion you now need to put them in numerical order. To do this proceed as follows:

a. Spread the pack to show the face-down cards spread throughout the face-up pack.

b. In doing this assume that the first face-down card you see is 1 less or 1 more in value than the card you noted at paragraph 3 above—1 less if the face-card of the selected suit was an Ace, and 1 more if the face-card of the selected suit was a King. Continue to spread the cards, mentally counting off the face-down cards as you come to them, counting **down** to the Ace if the face-card of the selected suit was an Ace, and **up** to the King if the face-card of the selected suit was a King. Irrespective of where you began the count note the position of the Ace or the King. When you have finished the spread cut the pack at that card to take it to what will be the bottom of the pack.

c. Now go through the pack again this time extracting the face-down cards in turn as you come to them, and placing them face-down in a pile on the table. As you go through the pack discard the face-up cards into a face-up pile on the table.

d. Now take the face down pile, turn it face-up, and deal out the selected suit in order.
(*Note: Depending upon the accuracy of your cut at paragraph 5 above the Ace will be either the first or last card in the sequence.*)

"Same Number, Same Card"

EFFECT

The picture or court cards are taken out of the pack. A spectator is asked to choose any one of them. It is placed face-up on the table and the spectator assigns to it any value from 1-10. The pack is then cut by the spectator and from the pack is then extracted a sequence of cards using the value given by the spectator to the court card at the start of the sequence. The total value of the extracted cards and the value of the court card is determined and a note is taken of this total and of the identity of the final card arrived at. The process is then repeated two more times. In every case the spectator allocates a different value to the court card. However, in every case the total arrived at and the final card of the sequence is the same.

PERFORMANCE

1. This trick is described in the chapter "*Old Wine In A New Bottle*". However, as it is an ideal trick to follow on from the previous trick "*All In Order*" it is appropriate to repeat it here. It can also be used following any trick which results in a numerical sequence of "10" to Ace or where such a sequence can be easily and secretly produced.
2. If you are using this trick as a follow-on trick from the trick "*All In Order*" you will have on the table a suit in numerical order Ace to King or "2" through King to Ace. Pick up all the cards on the table and re-constitute

them into a face-down pack, taking care to place the numerical sequence as the bottom cards of the face-down pack. Then cut the pack into two roughly equal packets and hand the top "half" to the spectator, instructing him or her to extract the picture or court cards from it. You do the same for your "half" of the pack, again ensuring that the numerical sequence "10" to Ace is positioned at the bottom of the packet when it is turned face-down. When both of you have extracted the court cards from your packets, take the packet from the spectator and place it on top of your own packet. Then instruct the spectator to cut and complete the pack. (*For an explanation of the term "cut and complete" see the "Introduction".*)

3. If you are performing the trick as a stand-alone trick where the necessary numerical sequence is not immediately available proceed as follows: shuffle the pack and then cut the pack into two roughly equal "halves". Hand one "half" to the spectator, who should extract the court cards, place them aside, and shuffle the remaining cards. Meanwhile, you extract the court cards from your "half" of the pack, place them aside, and, in doing so, as far as you are able, create a "10" to Ace sequence in the other cards. In discarding the court cards place them in a random face-up / face-down order. Take the shuffled cards from the spectator and hand him or her the face-up / face-down court cards. Instruct the spectator to go through them to ensure that there are no non-court cards in them. This should provide sufficient distraction to allow you to complete your "10" to Ace sequence and place it at the bottom of the face-down pack. You then place the pack face-down on the table and instruct the spectator to cut and complete it.

4. Now instruct the spectator to choose any one of the court cards, to place the chosen card face-up on the table, and to assign to it any value from 1 to 10. He or she should make a note of or remember this number.

5. You then take the pack and count off from the top of it a number of cards equal to the value the spectator has assigned to the court card. As the cards are counted their order is not reversed, ie. each card is counted off beneath the preceding card. The packet that is counted off is turned face-up to reveal the face card of the packet and the packet is then placed face-up on the court card so that only the left-hand index of the court card can be seen. You then use the value of the face card of the packet as the number of cards you next count off the top of the pack. This packet is placed on the preceding packet as described above and the process is continued through the pack until you reach the final card of the pack or until there are insufficient cards left in the pack to match the value of the face card of the packet.

6. The values of all the revealed cards and the value assigned to the initial face-up court card are now added together.

7. The spectator is instructed to note and remember this number and to note and remember the identity of the card arrived at.

8. Having arrived at this total, you collect up all the cards from left to right, sliding each card or packet beneath the subsequent card or packet, and then place the pack face-down on the table, or the cards you have collected up face-down on the face-down cards you have left over from the counting out.

9. Now repeat the process described in paragraphs 5-8 above, having forecast that you will arrive at the same

total and the same final card, and having allowed the spectator to assign a different number from 1 to 10 to the court card, which you take from the top of the pack and place face-up on the table. You will arrive at the same total and the same final card.

10. Collect up the cards as before, place the court card face-up on the table, and instruct the spectator to assign yet another value from 1 to 10 to it. Then go through the counting out procedure again and once again arrive at the same total and the same final card.

"The Next Turn"

Effect

After a series of shuffles and cuts of the pack the spectator selects a card and secretly notes its identity. The card is replaced in the pack which is again shuffled and cut. The performer then deals out the cards in a face-up line instructing the spectator not to give any indication when he or she sees the selected card. The performer continues the process until only one face-down card remains. He or she then states that the next card to be turned over will be the selected card (although the selected card has already been dealt out in the line of face-up cards). However, as the performer makes the statement he or she does not turn face-up the remaining face-down card. Instead he or she goes back along the line of cards and turns face-down the selected face-up card.

Performance

1. This is a quick trick that can be performed after any other trick that produces a suit in numerical sequence or when such a sequence can be secretly arranged.
2. To perform the trick take the sequence of 13 cards and invite the spectator to cut and complete the packet a number of times. Then take the packet and perform a Charlier Shuffle. *(For an explanation of "cut and complete" see the "Introduction" and for a description of how to perform the Charlier Shuffle see the chapter on "Handling and Sleights-of-Hand".)*

3. Next invite the spectator to shuffle the remaining cards of the pack.

4. Return now to the 13 cards used at paragraph 2 above and invite the spectator to take any one of them and to note its identity secretly. When he or she has done this instruct him or her to place his or her card at any position within the packet. This having been done, take the packet and give it a Charlier Shuffle, allowing the spectator to determine how many cards are transferred at each stage of the shuffle.

5. Now take the remaining cards of the pack, invite the spectator to cut them into two roughly equal piles, then to take the packet from paragraph 4 above and to cut that into two roughly equal piles. He or she may then reconstitute the pack in any way he or she wishes, placing the piles one upon another in any order. When that has been done, take the pack and perform a Charlier Shuffle. Finally, invite the spectator to cut the pack into two roughly equal packets. Take the packets and riffle shuffle them into each other. Having done this repeat the cutting and the shuffling once more. (*For a description of how to perform the riffle shuffle see the relevant section in the chapter "Handling and Sleights-of-Hand".*)

6. You now tell the spectator that you are going to deal out the pack and that while you are doing so you don't want any indication whatsoever as to the identity of his or her selected card. You then take the face-down pack and begin to deal out the cards from the top face-up into a pile on the table, placing the cards as they are dealt in an irregular pattern, ie so that no card completely covers the preceding card. As you are dealing out the cards mentally note the sequence in which the cards of the suit of the selected card are

appearing. At some point the sequence will be broken and the card breaking the sequence will be the selected card. (*NOTE: The sequence may be, for example, K–Q– A–2–3–4–5–6–J–7–8–9–10 or K–7–8–9–10–J–Q–A– 2–3–4–5–6. In the first sequence "J" would be the selected card and in the second sequence "K" would be the selected card.*

7. Irrespective of when you have noted the appearances of the selected card continue dealing out the cards until you have only one card left from the face-down pack. State then that the next card you turn over will be the card selected by the spectator. As you make this statement go through the cards on the table and turn face-down in front of the spectator the selected card.

"You Can Find It"

Effect

The pack is thoroughly shuffled and cut by the spectator and then by the performer. The performer deals out four cards face-down to the spectator, one of which the spectator selects and secretly notes. This card and the other three unchosen cards are returned to the pack, which is then shuffled. The spectator is next invited to cut the pack into two roughly equal packets and to look for the selected card in one of the packets and, when he or she does not find it, the performer hands the spectator the other packet and instructs him or her to deal off the top card of the packet face-up onto the table. The card is of the same value but not the same suit as the selected card. The next two cards that are dealt off face-up by the spectator are similarly of the same value as the selected card but not the same suit. The final card dealt out by the spectator is the selected card.

Performance

1. For its best effect this trick should be performed using a bridged card and sleights-of-hand. It can, however, be performed without the bridged card and sleights-of-hand and a description of how this is done is set out at paragraphs 10-14 below.
2. To perform the trick using the bridged card and sleights-of-hand begin by handing the face-down pack to the spectator and instructing him or her to give it a thorough shuffle. When he or she has done so, take the

pack back, place it face-down on the table and invite the spectator to cut it into two roughly equal packets. When this has been done take the two packets and riffle shuffle them together.

3. Having performed the shuffle, turn the pack face-up and begin to spread it, commenting upon the mix of the cards. In performing the spread what you are going to do is to cull or move four cards of the same identity (say, the "2s") to what will be the top of the pack when it is turned face-down. (*For a definition of the term "to cull" see the "Introduction" and for a description of how to perform the cull see the relevant section of the chapter "Handling and Sleights-of-Hand".*) Once the "2s" are in position at the top of the face-down pack, cut the bridged card from within the pack to place it at the bottom of the pack. (*For an explanation of how to do this see the relevant section of the chapter "Handling and Sleights-of-Hand".*)

4. You now have a face-down pack with the four "2s" as its top cards and the bridged card as its bottom card. Deal out face-down onto the table the top four cards of the pack, pick them up, mix their order, and invite the spectator to choose any one of them. He or she should make a secret note of its identity. You place the other three cards aside—still face-down.

5. You now invite the spectator to return the selected card to the "middle" of the face-down pack, and then cut and complete the pack. You then cut the bridged card to the bottom of the pack to place the selected card as the top card of the pack. (*For a definition of the term "cut and complete" see the "Introduction" and for details of how to use the bridged card in this handling see the relevant section of the chapter "Handling and Sleights-of-Hand".*)

6. Now take the three face-down cards you set aside at paragraph 4 above and, as instructed by the spectator, place them individually on the top or at the bottom of the face-down pack. When this has been done, perform a Charlier Shuffle and, finally, after the shuffle, cut the bridged card to the bottom of the pack. Immediately, cut the pack into two roughly equal packets and riffle shuffle the two packets together, ensuring that the top four cards of the pack remain as the top four cards of the pack. (*For descriptions of the Charlier Shuffle and how to control the riffle shuffle see the relevant sections of the chapter "Handling and Sleights-of-Hand".*)

7. Place the face-down pack on the table and instruct the spectator to cut off from the top of the pack about half the cards. When he or she has done so place the bottom "half" of the pack face-down in front of the spectator, and the "half" that has been cut off face-down in front of yourself. Having done so, instruct the spectator to cut the packet in front of you into two roughly equal packets.

8. You now instruct the spectator to go through the packet in front of him or her and find the selected card. As you are giving this instruction you place what was the bottom of the packet in front of yourself across what was the top of the packet.

9. When the spectator has discovered that the selected card is not in his or her packet comment that he or she might have better luck by taking the cards he or she cut to in the other packet. Take the cards that are across the top of this packet and place them aside. Hand the bottom cards to the spectator and instruct him or her to deal the top card face-up onto the table. It will be of the same value as the selected card but not the correct suit. The spectator may or may not comment on this. In

any case, get him or her to confirm it is not the selected card and to try again by dealing the next card face-up onto the table. This, again, will be the correct value of the card but, again, not the correct suit—as will be the next card he or she deals face-up from the pack. Finally, get him or her to deal face-up the fourth card which will be his or her selected card.

10. The crux of the trick is to produce an initial situation in which the spectator chooses one card from all four cards of the same value, eg. the "2s", or the "6s", or the "9s", etc. For its maximum effect the spectator should not be aware that he or she is selecting from "four of a kind", but, if it is not possible to achieve this, the trick, although weakened in its outcome, can be performed by allowing the spectator to choose with the cards openly displayed. Thus you would begin the trick by instructing the spectator to extract from the pack any four cards of the same value. However, there are ways in which you could secretly produce the necessary four cards as the top cards of a face-down pack without using any sleights-of-hand.

(1) The trick could be performed using the pack without the picture or court cards. This would require these cards to be extracted at the beginning of the trick thus providing you with the opportunity and distraction to make the necessary arrangement. To do this begin by handing "half" the pack to the spectator and instructing him or her to extract the court cards and to place them aside. You take the other "half" and do the same, taking the opportunity to collect as many cards of one "four of a kind" as you are able to at the top of your packet, say the "2s". In discarding the court cards place them in

a pile on the table, some face-up and some face-down. When both you and the spectator have gone through your packets, take the spectator's packet and place it at the bottom of your own packet. Then instruct him or her to sort out the court cards and check they are all there (there should be 12) while you check the pack. As you check the pack, if it is necessary, complete your "four of a kind" block of cards at the top of the face-down pack and, while you are doing this, also make a mental note of the bottom card of the face-down pack.

(2) The trick could be used as a follow-on trick from the trick "*Same Number, Same Card*" for the performance of which the court cards have already been extracted from the pack—11 of the court cards have been discarded and one of them (of which you know the identity) is at the top of the reconstituted face-down pack, say a Queen. Spread the court cards out face-up on the table and take one (*not* a Queen) and insert it face-down into the middle of the pack. Pick up another card (again *not* a Queen) and insert that card somewhere into the pack. Next pick up a Queen and place that card face-down on top of the pack. Take another card (of which you take a mental note, say Jack of Spades) and place that card at the bottom of the pack. Next take another card (*not* a Queen) and insert it within the pack, then take a Queen and place it at the bottom of the pack. This will leave you with five court cards on the table—one of which will be a Queen. Insert the cards which are not the Queen into the pack and place the Queen at the bottom of the pack. Then perform a Charlier Shuffle after which you should allow the spectator to cut and complete

the pack. (*For an explanation of the term "cut and complete" see the "Introduction" and for details on how to perform the Charlier Shuffle see the relevant section of the chapter "Handling and Sleights-of-Hand".*) This having been done, turn the pack face-up and spread it to show the mix of the cards. In performing this spread move the cards from right to left using the fingers of the left hand to pull the cards one above the other. At some point you will uncover the Jack of Spades. Immediately, place your left thumb on top of the next block of five or so cards to prevent them spreading and continue the spread by pulling the cards above them to the right with the right thumb. You then cut the spread to place the "Jack of Spades" as the bottom card of what will be the face down pack. In doing so, you will have placed the four Queens as the top four cards of the face-down pack.

11. By whatever way you have achieved it you now have either four "four of a kind" face-up cards on the table or four "four of a kind" face-down cards as the top cards of the face-down pack. If the former then turn them face-down and mix them; if the latter deal the top four cards face-down onto the table and mix them.
12. Now invite the spectator to take any one of the four cards and to note it secretly. While he or she is doing this, you should secretly note the bottom card of the face-down pack, and place the other three cards aside.
13. You now invite the spectator to return the selected card to the top or the bottom of the face-down pack. You then take the three cards you placed aside at paragraph 12 above and place them individually at the top or at the bottom of the pack as directed by the spectator.

Once this has been done, perform a Charlier Shuffle and then allow the spectator to cut and complete the pack. Finally, turn the pack face-up and spread it to show the mix of the cards. In doing this follow the procedure described at paragraph 10 above. (This will place the "four of a kind" as the top cards of the face-down pack with the selected card as the 4th card from the top of the pack.

14. Now proceed to bring the trick to its conclusion as described at paragraphs 7-9 above.

HANDLING AND
SLEIGHTS-OF-HAND

T HIS CHAPTER DEALS WITH the techniques that can be used
to manipulate and control the cards.

It is not intended that the newcomer to card magic
should work methodically through the material studying
and practising each technique. Such a procedure would not
only be counter-productive but also boring in the extreme.
Rather what is intended is that the reader should use the
chapter as a reference source on the various techniques,
turning to it as required during the study of the various
tricks and for this reason extensive references are made
to this chapter in the descriptions of the performance of
the tricks. However, the beginner is strongly advised to
master at the very outcome a number of essential skills.
These are:

The Overhand Shuffle and Controls
The Riffle Shuffle and Controls
A False Shuffle
A False Cut

With regard to the use of the techniques a word of warning is appropriate: do not over-use them. They do allow you to create the illusion of the cards being indiscriminately mixed. They do allow you to place cards in positions in a pack or packet that facilitate an effect. However, if they are used when they are not essential (either as a habit or to give you a degree of personal satisfaction in deluding the audience) their very use will give rise to suspicion and the spectators, seeing the moves used so often, will begin to look carefully at them and thus might detect the subterfuge involved.

Practice the techniques to the point at which they are almost automatic in performance and do not look at your hands when performing them. If you look at your hands the chances are that the spectators will too and what would go unobserved will be closely examined.

The Overhand Shuffle

Hold the pack face-down, with the outer end towards the spectators. The cards' outer sides should rest on the part of the palm at the junction between the palm and the fingers at an angle of about 45°, the inner side upward. The thumb rests across the top card of the pack, and the first finger is against the outer corner. The other fingers rest on the face of the bottom card.

Using the hand not holding the pack lift up the bottom half or so of the pack with the thumb holding the inner end of the packet and the first three fingers at the outer end.

Move the packet over the top of the other packet and pull off from the top of it single cards or clumps of cards with the thumb of the hand holding what was the top part of the pack, allowing the cards or single card to fall onto that packet as the packet in the other hand is moved backwards and forwards.

Carry on with this procedure until all the cards have been pulled off what was the bottom of the pack onto what was the top of the pack.

To continue the shuffle, again cut away the bottom half or so of the pack and go through the procedure gain.

CONTROLLING THE CARDS

The top card can be taken to the bottom of the pack by slipping the card off the top of the pack as the shuffle begins and immediately shuffling off the rest of the pack onto it, ie. the whole pack other than the top card is lifted to begin the shuffle.

The bottom card of the pack can be moved to the top of the pack by beginning the shuffle by lifting about the bottom $^2/_3$ of the pack. This packet is held between the thumb at the inner end and the second and third fingers at the outer end. As the shuffle progresses pressure is exerted on the final card in the packet to ensure that it is the final card shuffled off.

To hold the bottom card at the bottom of the pack the shuffle begins by lifting the packet which will be shuffled off from the middle of the pack and allowing the top and bottom remaining packets to fall together.

To transpose the top and bottom cards of the pack begin by slipping the top card as described above for taking the top card to the bottom. Then shuffle off all the other cards onto it exerting pressure on the final card (what was the bottom card of the pack) to ensure that this card is the final card shuffled off.

The Riffle Shuffle

Hold the pack face-down with the outer side of the pack towards the spectators. The pack is held with both hands, the thumbs at the inner side and the fingers at the outer side.

Split the pack into two halves, moving the top half to the left and the bottom half to the right, and place the two halves face-down on the table end to end, the outer sides of the packets still towards the spectators.

Move the two packets against each other until the two inner corners are touching and form the point a V with the open end of the V facing the spectators.

Change the position of the hands holding the packets so that the thumbs are immediately behind the corners forming the point of the V, the little fingers at the corners of the outside ends, the first fingers pressing down on the packets at the open part of the V. The little fingers are pushing at the end outside corners. The other fingers are at the outer sides of the packets.

Push down with all the fingers and at the same time lift the inner sides off the table with the thumbs, keeping the two corners forming the sharp end of the V in close contact.

Allow the cards to fall away in a cascade from the bottom of each packet interleaving with each other as they fall.

Close the V by pushing the inner ends of the two packets together thus completely inter-weaving them.

Push the two packets into each other and square up the pack.

CONTROLLING THE CARDS

To retain the top card or a top block of cards at the top of the shuffled pack control the release of the left hand packet (ie. what was the top half of the pack) so that the desired card or cards drop last.

To retain the bottom card or a bottom block of cards at the bottom of the shuffled pack allow the bottom card or the bottom cards of the right hand packet (ie. what was the bottom half of the pack) to fall first.

The Charlier Shuffle

With the outer ends of the cards facing the spectators, the pack is placed face-down diagonally across the up-turned palm immediately adjoining the base of the fingers. The thumb is at the outer side of the pack towards the outer corner and the tips of the fingers curl around the inner side.

The basic shuffle (or, rather, mix) begins by the other hand (palm down) moving over the pack. The thumb of this hand is at the inner end of the pack with the tip of the third finger curling over the outer end towards the inner corner. The pack is then tilted, the outer side of the pack pivoting on the upturned palm of the up-turned hand.

The upper hand now slides out a small packet of cards from the **bottom** of the pack, leaving the remainder of the pack resting on the fingers of the lower hand, the thumb of which moves onto the top of the pack.

This thumb now pushes off a small packet of cards from the **top** of what was the pack and these cards are slid **beneath** the cards held in the other (down-turned) hand.

The fingers of the up-turned hand now push off a small packet of cards from the **bottom** of what was the pack and these cards are placed on the **top** of the cards in the other (down-turned) hand.

This alternating top and bottom extraction of cards is continued until all the cards that constituted the original pack have been transferred and the shuffle (or mix) is complete. The rule to be remembered is that cards taken from the bottom go on top, and cards taken from the top go to the bottom.

CONTROLLING THE CARDS

Although the cards appear to have been thoroughly mixed the outcome of the shuffle is the same as would have resulted if the pack had been cut and completed. So, if at the end of the shuffle you cut the original bottom card of the pack back to the bottom of the pack then the pack will be back in its original order. Alternatively, if you had started with a bridged card at the bottom of the pack and if you cut it back to the bottom of the pack after the shuffle you would restore the pack to its original order.

Another method of controlling the mix when using a small packet of cards is to note the number of cards being transferred during the mix and then to perform a second mix transferring the same sequence of cards but this time starting the mix from the top of the pack. For example, if on the first mix of a 12-card packet you take four cards off the bottom, three off the top, two off the bottom, leaving three cards to be placed at the bottom and you then on the second mix take four cards off the top, three off the bottom, two off the top, leaving three cards to be placed on the top, the pack will be back in its original order. It might be thought that such handling would be immediately noted by the spectators but if it is done boldly and quickly it will be accepted as a fair mix of the pack.

Creating and Handling a
Bridged Card

There are a number of ways in which the bottom card of the pack may be handled to produce a convex bridge.

For the first, hold the pack face down with the outer end towards the spectators. The thumb is positioned on the outer side and the fingers wrap around the inner side. Move the other hand over the pack, the thumb at the inner end of the pack and the fingers at the outer end, and lift the pack very slightly, allowing the bottom card to fall onto and rest on the palm of the hand originally holding the pack, the separation of the card being facilitated by a slight upward pressure by the thumb of the upper hand on the rest of the pack, and the procedure being concealed by tilting the pack, ie. raising the inner end. Squeeze the card at its sides using the fingers of the lower hand to press the card against the fleshy part of the palm at the base of the thumb of the same hand. Only very slight pressure to produce a very slight bridge is required. Then allow the pack to drop back onto the card. The bottom card is bridged along its length with a convex bridge.

For the second, again hold the pack face-down with the outer end towards the spectators. The pack rests on the palm of the hand with the thumb at the outer side and the fingers wrapped around the inner side. The other hand moves over the pack and lifts it leaving the bottom card in the palm of the hand originally holding the pack. The pack is then turned so that the inner side points downwards towards the single card. The cards are then allowed to fall in a cascade onto the single card which is held between the fingers and thumbs of the lower hand. This will produce a "round of applause" (ie. the sound of cards falling onto the single card). More significantly, it produces a convex bridge of the card along its length.

A third method, which again allows you to bridge the card quite openly without raising any suspicion in the spectators, is to play with the pack in a very casual way while you are chatting with them. In doing so order the cards so that the card you wish to bridge is either the top card or bottom card of the face-down pack. When this has been achieved suddenly cut the pack into two roughly equal packets and hand the packet not containing the card you wish to bridge to a spectator, instructing him or her to shuffle it. While he or she is doing so you shuffle the packet you have retained to either take the top card to the bottom or the bottom card to the top and then back to the bottom, depending upon the initial position of the card you wish to bridge. At this point the spectator is likely to have completed his or her shuffle. Ask him or her to either give the packet another good shuffle or, if there is more than one spectator, to pass it to another spectator for them to shuffle. As this is being done turn your packet face-up and, while playing with the cards as you watch and chat with the spectator/s, take the top face-up card and, under cover of the hand not holding the packet, give that card a convex bridge along its length. Once you have done this cut the packet to place the bridged card roughly in the middle of the packet and turn the packet face-down. Now exchange packets with the spectator/s, instructing them to shuffle the second packet while you shuffle the other packet. The two packets are then placed together to reconstitute the pack (with somewhere within it your bridged card).

For some occasions (eg. a pre-prepared (or "stacked") trick of a routine) you are able to produce the bridged card prior to the performance in which you are going to use it. In which case, if the pre-prepared trick you are going to use it for allows it, once you have created the bridged card cut it into the middle of the pack before placing the pack in its carton.

You should note that only a very slight bridge is required to produce the desired outcome and that during performance (particularly after riffle shuffles) it may be necessary to "refresh" the bridge.

HANDLING A BRIDGED CARD

To cut the bridged card from within the pack hold the pack loosely, the outer end towards the spectators, with the face of the cards facing outwards and the backs inwards. The thumb is very loosely on the top side of the pack and the fingers are gently supporting the bottom side from beneath. The other hand (again very gently) rests on the pack, the thumb at the inside end and the fingers at the outer end. The pressure of the thumb on the top side of the pack is relaxed, and the pack is allowed to open at the natural break. The bottom section of the pack will fall into the palm of the hand. You lift away this bottom packet of the pack and place it face-down on top of the pack. This should put the bridged card to the bottom of the re-constituted pack. It is prudent, however, to check that this has been achieved and this can be done by glimpsing the card at the bottom of the pack. To do this, after you have completed the cut, turn the face-down pack so that the backs of the cards are towards the spectators with the sides of the cards at top and bottom. Hold the pack with both hands, the back of the hands towards the spectators and with the thumbs on the face of the pack and the fingers on the back of the pack. Tap the bottom side of the pack on the table to square up the cards and, in doing so, glimpse the identity of the bottom card. Once you have done so turn the pack face-down and place it on the table. If you do not glimpse the required card have the pack cut again or cut the pack yourself and repeat the whole procedure.

To allow the pack to be cut and to then restore it to its original order begin with the bridged card at the bottom of the face-down pack and allow the pack to be cut and completed. Then cut the bridged card to the bottom of the pack as described in the previous paragraph. To control a selected card which has been returned to either the top or the bottom of the pack after the pack has been cut and completed begin with the bridged card at the bottom of the pack and allow a spectator to replace his or her selected card on the top or at the bottom of the pack. Then allow the spectator to cut and complete the pack as many times as he or she wishes. If you then cut the bridged card to the bottom of the pack the selected card will be the top card of the pack.

To control a selected card returned to the "the middle of the pack" after the pack has been cut and completed begin with the bridged card at the bottom of the pack. Cut off the top half of the face-down pack and place it face-down on the table in front of the spectator. He or she places the selected card on top of this packet and you place what was the bottom half of the pack on top of the selected card. The spectator may now cut and complete, at will. Finally, you cut the bridged card to the bottom of the pack, which places the selected card at the top of the pack. Alternatively, with the pack in hand, cut off the top half of the pack with the other hand and hold this packet face-down towards the spectator for him or her to place the selected card on top of it. Then place what was the bottom of the pack face-down on top of the spectator's card. You then proceed as described above, allowing the spectator to cut and complete before you finally cut the bridged card to the bottom of the pack.

To disguise the use of a bridged card or to retain a card or block of cards at the top of the pack, having cut the bridged card to the bottom of the pack begin the procedure again. This time, in relaxing the pressure of the thumb on the top side of the pack, allow approximately the bottom $1/_3$ of the pack to fall away into the palm. Now using the index finger of the other hand you open the top $2/_3$ of the pack as if opening a book and insert what was the bottom $1/_3$ of the pack into the gap thus formed and then close the pack. The bridged card is now approximately $2/_3$ of the way down the pack. Repeat this procedure allowing the cards **below** the bridged card to fall into the palm of your hand. As you did before, open up a gap in the other cards and place the cards from your palm in it. When the pack is closed the bridged card will be at the bottom of the pack.

False Shuffles

The simplest false shuffle is what is normally described as the "optical shuffle". If it is performed confidently and smoothly, without looking at the hands or attracting the attention of the spectators to the hands, it is a very deceptive false shuffle. To perform it begin with the pack in position for an overhand shuffle as described earlier in this chapter. Cut away about the bottom $2/_3$ of the pack and, as in the genuine overhand shuffle, move this packet over the top of the other packet. Do so until it completely covers the other packet without relaxing your grip of it. As the cut-away packet moves over the packet that was the top of the pack place the thumb of the hand holding this packet on top of the cut-off packet, then take the bottom $2/_3$ you cut-off upwards, as you do so allowing the thumb to slip along the top card of the upward moving packet **but do not release any cards from the packet**. Once the packet has cleared what was the bottom $1/3$ of the pack move it down behind that packet and allow a small block of cards to fall onto the bottom of that packet. Continue the procedure until all the cards from what was the bottom part of the pack have been placed behind what was the top $1/3$ of the pack. The illusion of a true shuffle can be heightened by, when the $2/3$ packet is moved behind the $1/3$ packet, the cards of the $1/3$ packet are allowed to tilt towards the thumb of the hand holding them.

Another straight-forward and effective false shuffle again begins with the cards in the position for an overhand shuffle. Take about the bottom ¾ of the pack and lift it above the other cards as if beginning a standard overhand shuffle. At the same time the thumb of the lower hand pulls the top ¼ of the pack down onto the fingers of that hand and moves this packet under what was the bottom ¾ of the pack. A break or gap is held between what was the upper ¼ of the pack and what was the bottom ¾ of the pack using the thumb and fingers of the hand holding the pack. Continue pulling of small blocks of cards from the top of what was the bottom ¾ of the pack, placing these blocks beneath what was the top ¼ of the pack, maintaining the gap or break. When all the cards have been transferred the pack will be back in its original order. The secret of success with this false shuffle (which is, in fact, a series of cuts off the top of the pack being transferred to the bottom of the pack in order) is to keep the gap or break as small as possible and to hide it with what was the bottom ¾ of the pack by tilting the pack towards the spectators. The illusion created is of the cards being shuffled into the bottom part of the pack.

False Cuts

If you are using a bridged card the illusion of a fair cut is easily achieved (beginning with the bridged card at the bottom of the pack) by casually cutting and completing the pack two or more times before cutting the bridged card to the bottom of the pack. If, however, you are not using a bridged card or if the bridged card is and must remain within the pack then the illusion must be achieved by other means. One straight-forward (but still deceptive) procedure is to begin with the pack face-down with the outer side towards the spectators. The pack is held with both hands, the thumbs at the inner side and the fingers at the outer side. Tilt the pack, raising the inner side with the thumbs, and then with the right hand pull the bottom $1/_3$ of the pack to the right and place it face down on the top of the pack, out-jogged on the outer end of the pack by about half an inch. The consequent out-jog at the inner end of the pack is concealed by the back of the left hand. Repeat the movement for the next $1/_3$ of the pack from the bottom of the pack—this time placing the cut-off packet directly on top of the out-jogged packet. Now push down with the left little finger on what is the concealed out-jogged bottom $1/_3$ of the packet and pull that packet to the right under the pack with the right hand, placing it on the top of the pack. The pack is then in its original order. The procedure when performed quickly and slickly gives the illusion of a genuine cut.

A False Mix of the Pack

The impression can be given that a pack or block of cards is being thoroughly mixed when, in fact, no change is being made in its order. To do this begin with a bridged card at the bottom of the pack or packet and by then performing a Charlier Shuffle as described earlier in this chapter. You may, if you wish, during the shuffle allow a spectator to determine how many cards you take from the top and from the bottom of the pack or packet. Having completed the shuffle you place the pack face-down on the table, cut off the top ¾ of the pack, and place this packet by the side of what was the bottom of the pack (A). Now cut off the top ¾ of the packet you took off A and place these cards by the side of what was this packet (B). Now cut off the top half of the packet you have placed beside B and place it by the side of what was the bottom of this packet (C). The last packet is D. You now have on the table four packets D – C – B – A. Place A on D and B on AD and then invite a spectator to determine whether C is placed on top of or beneath BAD. Do as he or she wishes and then perform a second Charlier Shuffle. Both you and the spectators may now cut and complete, at will. Finally, you cut the bridged card to the bottom of the pack and the pack is then back in its original order.

The mix may be made without using a bridged card if the bottom card of the pack at the beginning of the procedure is secretly noted. Then at the end of the procedure the pack is turned face-up and spread to show the mix of the cards. When the pack is cut to place the noted card at what will be the bottom of the face-down pack then the pack will have been restored to its original order (*see the section on "Using A Key Card" later in this chapter.*)

The Double Lift

The generally accepted method of performing a double lift is to begin with the outer end of the pack or packet facing the spectators. The cards are held across the palm of the hand with the thumb along the outer side, extending just a little beyond the corner. The four fingers curl around the inner side of the cards. The other hand (palm down) moves over the cards, the fingers at the outer end, the thumb at the inner end. This allows the thumb of this hand to lift the top two cards of the pack or packet to form a small break at the inner end, and this break is immediately taken up by the little finger of the lower hand. At this stage, if it is so wished, the upper hand may be removed and the pack or packet displayed without revealing the break, particularly if when the pack or packet is displayed the outer end is slightly raised.

The lift is made by the thumb of the hand holding the cards sliding from its position at the outer corner to a position on top of the pack or packet, pressing down the middle of the top card. As this movement is being made the other hand (palm down) moves over the cards taking up the same position as described in the previous paragraph. In a combined movement the thumb of the lower hand begins to push the top two cards towards the inner side of the pack or packet while the fingers and thumb of the upper hand assist the movement exerting sufficient pressure to maintain the two cards in alignment. The illusion created is that only one card (the top card) is being moved. In fact, the top two cards are being moved as one. The thumb of the lower hand continues to exert a downward pressure on the middle of the cards.

When the two cards (aligned as one) have been moved approximately half-way across the pack or packet the upper hand is turned palm-up. The fingers of the upper hand now move to beneath the top two cards (still aligned as one) and the thumb of this hand moves to the top of the two cards. The top two cards are then being held in alignment and on the pack by the fingers and thumb of the upper hand, allowing the thumb of the lower hand to slide off the cards onto the top of the other cards of the pack or packet. The cards continue to be moved across the pack or packet and sufficient pressure is exerted on them to produce a convex curve to the face of the cards. As the cards reach the end of the movement across the pack or packet they will abut against the fingers of the lower hand, which are used as a fulcrum to allow the two cards (still aligned as one) to be flipped over and dropped as one onto the cards being held in the lower hand. This will display the face of the second card.

The whole process is now repeated to place the cards back face-down on the pack or packet.

The position that has now been achieved is that the spectator believes that the top face-down card of the pack or packet is what is in fact the second card from the top of the pack or packet, and the performer may take whatever advantage he or she wishes from this misconception.

The essence of the illusion is to ensure that the two cards are maintained in perfect alignment throughout the whole procedure.

A second method of performing the double lift, although less natural, ensures that any mis-alignment on the initial lift is hidden from the spectator. Using this method you begin with the cards in exactly the same position as in the method already described. However, in this second method, once the thumb of the upper hand has secured the break at the inner end of the pack or packet, the inner ends of the top two cards (aligned as one) are lifted by the thumb about ½" off the pack. At the same time the fingers of this hand move onto the top of the two cards, firmly pressing the outer ends of the cards down on the top of the pack, and then pulling the cards along the length of the pack. When the cards have been pulled approximately half-way along the top of the pack they are turned over as one still maintaining their movement along the pack until what was the outer end of the two cards is a little beyond the inner end of the pack. Throughout this movement the fingers of the lower hand and the thumb of the lower hand maintain the alignment of the two cards at the sides and the fingers of the upper hand maintain the alignment of the cards at their outer end by the pressure they are exerting on the cards. The thumb of the upper hand maintains the alignment of the inner end of the cards. The thumb of the upper hand now slides along the top of the cards to pick up the slight extension of the two cards at the inner end of the pack while the fingers of this hand maintain the alignment of the outer end. You should note that, throughout, the position of the fingers and thumb of the upper hand hide any possible mis-alignment of the ends from the spectators, and the thumb and fingers of the lower hand hide any mis-alignment at the sides. You are now in a position to turn the two cards face-down on the pack using the same procedure as described above for the initial turn. However, if so wished, they may be turned face-down using the turn-over described in the first version of the lift.

If the trick being performed requires it, it is possible to lift three, or even four cards, as one. However, the more cards that are lifted the more their alignment (and thickness) becomes problematical and the more likely it is that the spectator will detect the subterfuge. Nevertheless, the double lift (if not over-used) is a most powerful tool for creating some very strong effects.

Using A Key Card

A key card is used to allow the performer to locate and, if necessary, to manipulate the position of an unknown card placed in the pack by a spectator. If it is used to locate and identify the unknown card the performer ensures that when the unknown card is placed in the pack the key card (of which the performer knows the identity) is placed next to it or in a known proximity to it. The manipulations required to allow this to be done are the same as are described for handling a bridged card when a selected card is placed in "the middle of the pack" and when the key card is the original bottom card of the face-down pack. What is then required to identify the unknown card is for the performer to spread the cards face-up to show the mix of the cards and to identify the unknown card by its position in relation to the key card. The manipulation to move the now identified card to a position advantageous for the performer is again achieved as with a bridged card, ie. the pack is cut so that the key card will be the bottom card of the pack when the pack is turned face-down. This will place the selected card as the top card of the face-down pack.

The essential skill required by the performer is the ability to spread and cut the pack when it is face-up without arousing any suspicion in the spectator. If the cards are spread from right to left with the thumb of the right hand, pushing each card under the preceding card, then the selected card will be immediately above the key card and must be quickly pulled out of view under the preceding cards. If the cards are spread from right to left as described paragraph 9e for the trick "Card Sharper's Aces", sliding the cards with the fingers of the left hand from the bottom of the pack with each card moving above the preceding card, then the key card will be located first and the selected card can be hidden by suppressing it in the spread. In this case, of course, the performer will not be able to identify the selected card. He or she will, however, be able to position it as the top card of the face-down pack.

The Cut Deeper Force

To force a card is, by concealed means, to ensure that a spectator receives or chooses a card or cards determined by the performer. A straight-forward, yet very effective, force for the top card of the pack, as developed by the card magician Ed Balucci, is the Cut Deeper Force. The force is accomplished by first cutting off about ¼ of the pack, turning this packet over, and placing it on top of the rest of the pack. The pack is then cut about ½ way down and this packet is turned over and placed on top of the other cards. The first face-down card in the pack is what was originally the top card of the pack. The deceptiveness of the procedure can be enhanced by allowing the spectator to make all the cuts.

The principle underlying the procedure can be adapted to meet any requirement. For example, if the top ¼ of the pack is cut off, turned over, and placed beneath the rest of the pack, and then the bottom ½ of the pack is cut-off, turned over, and placed on top of the pack, what was originally the bottom card of the pack will be the first face-up card in the pack. This procedure could be used at the conclusion of a trick to reveal a spectator's selected card that has been manipulated to the bottom of the pack.

Further variations of the principle are used in the trick *"Everybody Shouts"* when performed without the use of a bridged card (*see the previous chapter*). In the second variation the procedure is varied to force the bottom card of the pack **face-down**.

Magician's Choice

Magician's Choice (or, as it is sometimes referred to by the French word meaning ambiguous—"equivoque") is a means of producing the outcome in a spectator's choice of card or cards that is required by the performer. Its success depends upon the way in which the choice is presented to the spectator and the way in which the response is interpreted by the performer.

An example of a multiple choice illustrates the principle involved.

You begin by placing five cards or five packets of cards on the table—say A, B, C, D, and E, with A being the required card or packet. The spectator is asked to "pick out" any four cards or packets and to touch the cards or packets. If the spectator chooses B, C, D, and E you pick up those cards or packets and place them aside, leaving you with the required card or packet. If the spectator chooses A and three other cards or packets discard the card or packet he has not chosen and proceed to another choice. You now have on the table A and, say, B, C, and D, and you ask the spectator "now to choose any two of the four that are left". If the spectator chooses any two of B, C, or D discard those cards or packets, leaving A and one other card or packet. If the spectator chooses A and another card or packet, discard the other two cards or packets, again leaving A and one other card or packet. You now have A and one other card or packet on the table and you now ask the spectator "to pick out one of those cards / packets". If he chooses A then you discard the other card or packet. If he chooses the other card or packet you discard that. In any case, you finish with the required card on the table.

Transferring Bottom Card to Top

The most effective way to transfer the bottom card to the top of the pack is by an overhand shuffle (*see the relevant section earlier in this chapter*). However, it is possible to make the transfer by means of a cut. To do so begin with the face-down pack diagonally across the palm with the outer end towards the spectators. The pack should be tilted roughly at an angle of about 45° with the inner end raised. The thumb is at the outer side corner and the fingers wrap around the inner side from below, the little finger at the inner side corner. The other hand (palm down) is over the top of the pack with the fingers at the outer end and the thumbs at the inner end. The little finger of the lower hand pulls down on the inner corner of the bottom card of the pack to form a break (*for an explanation of this term see the "Introduction"*). As soon as the break is formed it is transferred immediately to the fleshy part of the top of the thumb of the upper hand as the bottom hand moves slightly outwards and away from the pack. This bottom hand now turns palm towards the outer side of the pack and using the middle finger at the outer end of the pack and the thumb at the upper end extracts the middle third of the pack. As the packet is extracted it rests on the third and little finger and the index finger presses down on the packet. This grip allows the thumb to move onto the top of the packet to replace the index finger which moves to below the cards. The packet is now gripped by the thumb on top and all the fingers below. The fingers move under the packet to wrap around the inner side as the thumb slides to the outside corner—the packet now lies diagonally across the palm of the hand. The other (upper) hand now places its packet face-down on top of the packet. As it does so the thumb of the upper hand allows the card below the break to drop onto the lower packet, the card being guided onto the packet by the thumb and fleshy part of the palm below the thumb of the lower hand. Simultaneously, the thumb of the upper hand forms and holds a break at the inner end of the pack between the packet it holds and the bottom packet.

The lower hand now moves away from the pack and then, turning palm towards the outer side of the pack, removes a block of cards from the middle of the pack above the break held by the thumb. This block of cards is placed on top of the pack. The cards that were below the break are then transferred to the top of the pack, which is then placed face-down on the table.

An alternative and much easier way to accomplish the same outcome is to use a Charlier-style mix. If it is used it should be done boldly and quickly, if possible while providing some distraction of the attention of the spectators. The handling required begins with the pack in position as for a "genuine" Charlier Shuffle or mix (*see the relevant section earlier in this chapter*). The cards are pushed off by the thumb from the top of the pack. They are pushed off individually under the previous card until a small block is formed. This packet is then taken by the other hand **on top of** the cards already taken off. This procedure continues through the pack, **the cards all being taken from the top of the pack**, alternating the placing of the packets above and below the cards already taken off. At the end of the procedure a small packet (of, say, 5 or 6 cards) is left of the original pack. All but the last of these cards are transferred below the cards already taken off and the last card is placed on top of the pack. The pack is then placed on the table.

Transferring Top Card to Bottom

Again the most effective way to transfer the card is by an overhand shuffle (*see the relevant section earlier in this chapter*), but also again it can be accomplished by a cut or a mix.

To perform the cut begin with the pack held as for the cutting procedure described in the previous section except that for this procedure the outer end of the pack should be slightly raised, and the break should be formed and held below the top card of the pack. Cut off the bottom ¼ of the pack and place these cards on top of the pack. Still holding the break cut off what is now the bottom ¼ of the pack and place these on top. Then take all the cards below the break and place these on top. End the cut by taking out about $^1/_3$ of the pack from the middle and playing these cards on top.

To accomplish the same outcome by means of a Charlier-style mix reverse the procedure described in the previous section, ie. the cards are taken from the bottom of the pack and the last card of the final packet is placed below the cards taken off.

Culling A Card Or Cards

The ability to cull or extract a card secretly from within the pack to move it to a more advantageous position (usually the top of the face-down pack) opens up many opportunities for the performer of card magic.

The handling by which such a cull is achieved begins by turning the pack face-up with the outer end towards the spectators, the pack tilting slightly downward towards them. The pack is held with both hands (palms up)—the fingers beneath the cards and the thumbs on the face of the cards.

Ostensibly to show the mix of the cards, you then begin to spread the pack, pushing the cards either right to left with the right thumb or left to right with the left thumb, each card as it is pushed along moving beneath the preceding card. The spread as it progresses rests on the fingers of the receiving hand. When you see the card you wish to place at the top of the face-down pack the first or index finger of the receiving hand moves onto the face of that card as it is pushed along (ie, the nail of the finger makes contact above the advancing side of the card). This places the fingers of the receiving hand at the back of the selected card and, while the spread continues, the card is drawn towards the outside edge of the receiving packet. Simultaneously, the packet from which the cards are being pushed is moved very slightly upwards, sufficient only to allow the tips of the fingers of the pushing hand to open up a small gap between the selected card and the receiving packet. Once this has been done the cards as they are pushed across the spread will move over the selected card—and the first finger of the receiving hand can move back to its position below the selected card. The spread can then be cut at any subsequent point, which will place the selected card at the top of the pack when the pack is turned face-down, or the whole pack can be spread producing the same result.

To cull a number of cards from within the pack to the top of the pack begin as you would in culling a single card as described above. Once the first card you wish to cull is in position beneath the cards in the receiving hand and the subsequent cards of the spread are being pushed above it, insert the tip of the fingers of the pushing hand above the first selected card. This will ensure that the small gap between the selected card and the receiving packet is maintained and allow the fingers of the receiving hand to fix the selected card in position beneath the spread. When you come to the next card you wish to cull withdraw the tips of the fingers from the gap. At the same time, using the thumb of the pushing hand, fix one or two cards preceding it in the spread, and, using the fingers of the remaining hand, pull the selected card underneath them and to the outside edges of the receiving packet. In doing this the selected card will move beneath the previously selected card and will move clear of the cards that have been fixed by the pushing thumb. As the spread is continued the cards that were fixed will move above the first selected card and the fingers of the pulling hand are able to restore that gap above it. The process continues in this way until all the required cards are in position.

SOURCES AND BACKGROUND

I OWE MY OWN INTEREST in card magic to the writers mentioned in the *"Introduction"* to this book and included in the short bibliography set out below, and, as will be obvious in the section that follows, the development of the tricks in this book would not have been possible without drawing heavily on their work. I take this opportunity to express my admiration of their contribution to the advancement of card magic and to express my gratitude to them for the pleasure and inspiration they have given to me over many years.

A Basic Reference Library

Jean Hugard and Frederick Braué
The Royal Road to Card Magic (Dover, New York, 1999)
Expert Card Technique (Dover, New York, 1974)
Jean Hugard and John J. Crimmins, Jnr
The Encyclopaedia of Card Tricks (Dover, New York, 1974)

(a revised edition with Index was published by Foulsham, Slough, 2003)

Karl Fulves

Self-Working Card Tricks (Dover, New York, 1976)

More Self-Working Card Tricks (Dover, New York, 1984)

Self-Working Close-up Card Magic (Dover, New York, 1995)

Self-Working Mental Magic (Dover, New York, 1979)

Martin Gardner

Mathematics, Magic, and Mystery (Dover, New York, 1956)

And for those who wish to develop further their repertoire and techniques the following books are recommended:

Arthur F. MacTier

Card Concepts (Davenport, London, 2000)

Simon Aronson

Bound To Please (Aronson, Chicago, 1994)

The Background to the Tricks

This section discusses the principles and the mechanics underpinning the tricks and, where appropriate, acknowledges the sources which provided the initial inspiration for the effect or suggested the means by which particular effects could be achieved.

"MAGIC ACES"

"Finding The Aces"

This trick is composed of a series of forces based on the fact that if you take a block of cards and cut off from it 10 to 19 cards, count out those cards reversing their order, and then go to the card in the counted-out cards corresponding to the number derived by adding the two digits of the counted-out number together, then the card arrived at will be the card that was the 10th from the top in the original block of cards.

A few calculations illustrate the principle involved:

$(10 = 1 + 0 = 1)$ and $(10 - 1 = 9)$
$(15 = 1 + 5 = 6)$ and $(15 - 6 = 9)$
$(18 = 1 + 8 = 9)$ and $(18 - 9 = 9)$

In other words the number of cards remaining in the block of cards after the second count will always be nine, and these cards will be the original top nine cards of the block.

The forcing of the first Ace in the trick is a straightforward application of this principle.

The forcing of the second Ace is an application of the same principle with the performer controlling the size of the block of cards removed.

The principle can be extended to allow for blocks of cards larger than 19 to be used. However, in these cases the position of the card to be forced has to be appropriately adjusted, the reason being that the underlying principle is that for any two digit number if the two digits are added together and the single digit figure arrived at is subtracted from the original number then the final number arrived at will always be a multiple of 9.

Again a few calculations illustrate this:

$(23 = 2 + 3 = 5)$ $(23 - 5 = 18)$ $(9 \times 2 = 18)$
$(35 = 3 + 5 = 8)$ $(35 - 8 = 27)$ $(9 \times 3 = 27)$
$(47 = 4 + 7 = 11)$ $(47 - 11 = 36)$ $(9 \times 4 = 36)$

Again the multiple of 9 will always be the number of cards remaining in the block after the second count. Thus in a block of 20-29 cards the card to be forced requires to be at the 19th position from the top in the original block, in a block of 30-39 cards at the 28th position, and in a 40-49 block at the 37th position.

The forcing of the third Ace in the trick follows from the fact that at the beginning of the second force there are 19 cards above the third Ace. 18 of these cards are returned to the top of the pack and these cards remain in hand on the force:

$(25 = 2 + 5 = 7)$ and $(25 - 7 = 18)$
$(27 = 2 + 7 = 9)$ and $(27 - 9 = 18)$
$(29 = 2 + 9 = 11)$ and $(29 - 11 = 18)$

It would be possible to force the fourth Ace using the same principle but three forces using the same procedure are enough and, in any case, the arrangement for the fourth Ace to be produced from the bottom of the pack provides just as strong, perhaps even stronger, a finish.

A full description of the straight-forward Four Card Force can be found at page 188 of the book "*Expert Card Techniques*" (Dover Publications Inc., New York, 1974) by Jean Hugard and Frederick Braué, and readers who wish to study further the uses to which mathematical principles can be put in card magic are recommended to see the books *"Card Concepts"* (Lewis Davenport, London, 2004) by Arthur F. MacTier and Martin Gardner's *"Mathematics, Magic, and Mystery"* (Dover Publications Inc., New York, 1956). In this latter book the reader will be interested to note at page 20 a description of a trick in which the principle used for my trick *"Finding The Aces"* is applied in a different way. It is a four Ace trick, ascribed by Martin Gardener to Billy O'Connor, where, before the performance begins, the Aces are secretly placed at the 9th, 10th, 11th, and 12th positions from the top of the pack. The performer then invites a spectator to choose any number between 10 and 20 and, once this number has been chosen, he or she deals out that number of cards face-down onto the table from the top of the face-down pack. The two digits of the chosen number are then added together to give a single digit number and the number of cards corresponding to this number are dealt off the top of the pile onto the table. These cards are then placed on top of the pack. When the top card of **the pile** is turned over the first Ace is revealed. It is removed from the pile and placed on the table. The performer then places what were the remaining cards of the dealt-out pile on top of the pack and continues the trick, going through the same procedure to reveal the second, then the third, and then the fourth Ace. The handling and the secret positioning of the Aces, of course, ensure that when the cards corresponding to the calculated number are returned to the pack there will always be 9 cards on the table, and the top card of this pile will be an Ace.

"You Must Be Joking"

This trick combines a number of ways of handling the cards to produce a surprising and amusing effect. The impression created is that the cards are being thoroughly mixed, particularly when the cards are riffle shuffled together. In fact, neither the cutting of the cards nor the shuffles in any way alters the position of the Aces or the Jokers in relation to each other.

The riffle shuffle is a most useful handling device in card manipulation in that when the two parts of the pack are inter-weaved the order of the cards in the two parts is maintained. In addition, the shuffle allows the performer to retain cards at the top and/or at the bottom of the pack as he or she wishes. Both these characteristics of the shuffle are fully utilised in the performance of the trick to control the location of the Aces and the Jokers within the pack.

For some interesting uses to which the riffle shuffle can be put the reader may care to see Karl Fulves' book *"More Self-Working Card Tricks"* (Dover Publications Inc., New York, 1984, pages 45-56).

"Card Sharper's Aces"

This is a mini-routine in its own right combining a number of tricks drawing their inspiration from several sources.

The first part of the trick involving the initial dealing out of the Aces is based on the classic *"Three Jack Deal"*. This is described in three versions by Karl Fulves in his book *"Self-Working Close-Up Card Magic"* (Dover Publications Inc., New York, 1995) at pages 75-79: *"Jack, Jack, Jack"*, *"Three Jacks Improved"*, and *"Unstacked Jacks"*.

There are some intrinsic weaknesses in the basic trick as described in *"Jack, Jack, Jack"*. The first is that the trick requires a pre-arrangement of five cards, ie., Jack, Jack, Jack, any card, Jack, at the top of the pack; the second is that it is necessary to use the subterfuge of "scooping up" the dealer's undisplayed cards using the last undisplayed card dealt to ensure that when those cards are placed back on top of the pack with the spectator's displayed Jacks placed face-down on them the original pre-arrangement is re-created; and the third is that when the performer goes to the second deal the colour combination of the revealed Jacks may differ from deal to deal, e.g. if the first deal produced Red-Red-Black the second deal will produced Black-Black-Red, which is unlikely not to give the spectator a strong inkling as to how the effect is being achieved. To an extent, the *"Three Jacks Improved"* version of the trick, the development of which Fulves ascribes to Walter Gibson, obviates this weakness by ensuring that the only change between the first and second deal is the identity of the Black Jack, but this only at the expense of a more complicated pre-arrangement of the top cards of the pack, ie. Red Jack, Black Jack, Red Jack, any card, Black Jack and an even more complicated subterfuge for picking up the cards to arrange them for the second deal in that in addition to the handling used in the "*Jack, Jack, Jack*" version to place the Jack of the three undisplayed dealer's cards as the middle card of the three, the same handling is used to place the Black Jack of the spectator's three displayed Jacks in the middle of those cards. Jack Potter's version of the trick, to which Fulves gives the title "*Unstacked Jacks*" requires no pre-arrangement of the pack other than placing one Black Jack as the third card in the pack while openly displaying the other three Jacks. Six cards are then inter-leaved by placing the first face-down card from the top of the pack face-down on the table, by then placing the revealed Black Jack face-down on top of it, and by then carrying on this procedure for the two Red Jacks. If these six cards are then placed on top of the pack and the top three cards are dealt out face-up onto the table, they will be two Red Jacks and one Black Jack. Furthermore, if these Jacks (with the Black Jack as the middle card of the three) are replaced face-down on top of the pack then the top cards are set for the "*Jack, Jack, Jack*" version of the trick. The weakness remaining, of course, is that the identify of the Black Jack will still alter from deal to deal. Accepting this weakness, it is on Jack Potter's version of the trick that I have based my own.

There is, however, yet another weakness in all the version of the trick as described by Fulves which is that at no time during the performance of the trick are all six cards displayed (or rather, apparently displayed) to the spectator. My own version, using the double lift to conceal the second Black Ace, is a means of over-coming this weakness. Furthermore, in my version of the trick no subterfuge is required to re-set the pre-arrangement for the second deal.

The second part of the trick, the dealing out of the Poker hands, is set up by demonstration of how the hands will be dealt. This places the Aces in a configuration to allow the spectator a free choice of cards in the actual deal. On the assumption that it might be of interest and use to the reader a method that can be used to determine the required pre-arrangement is set out below:

ORDER	1	2	3	4	5	6	7	8	9	10
CARD	X	A	X	A	A	X	X	X	X	A

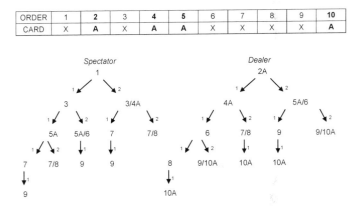

"Telepathic Aces"

This trick depends for its success on the method used to identify the cards around which the Aces are placed in the Miniature pack or in the first full-sized pack if the Miniature pack is not used.

The method is usually referred to as "*the pump action*", "*the push-pull effect*", or "*the piston effect*" and it is normally used by the performer to produce a selected card rising from within the pack. Here, however, the effect is reversed and concealed to allow the performer to identify a card.

The use of the piston effect to produce a rising card is attributed in most books on card magic to Jack McMillen.

"Just Think of An Ace"

Spelling out a selected card always creates a strong impression on spectators, spelling out a card that has only been thought of by a spectator even more so. The trick *"Just Think of An Ace"*, which does this, is based on the fortunate fact that the number of letters in the spelling out of the Aces can be manipulated to produce a sequence: "Ace of Clubs" (10), "Ace of Hearts" (11), "Ace of Diamonds" (13). Thus any one of them can be spelled out by taking the card placed at the appropriate position of the final "s" of the spelling. "Ace of Spades" (11) can be accommodated into the sequence by placing it between "Ace of Hearts" (11) and "Ace of Diamonds" (13) and by taking the card left on the top of the pack when "Ace of Spades" is spelled out, ie. the 12th card. The essence of the trick therefore becomes the handling required to place the Aces in their appropriate positions.

A version of this trick under the title *"Think of An Ace"* is also used in the routine described in the chapter *"Old Wine In A New Bottle"*.

"All Together Again"

This trick is based on a principle developed by Simon Aronson and described in his book *"Bound To Please"* (Aronson, Chicago, 1994). It is also discussed by Arthur F. MacTier in his *"Card Concepts"* (Davenport, London, 2000). The principle is that if a pack of cards is divided into two packets and if a number of cards from each packet are turned over and shuffled into the other packet and this process is repeated as many times as wished, then, if, finally, one of the packets is turned over and shuffled into the other packet, the pack will contain the original two packets, one face-up and the other face-down.

In the trick *"All Together Again"* the Aces constitute a face-down packet and the rest of the cards a face-up packet. The fact that the packet contains cards with differently coloured backs significantly heightens the impression that the pack is being thoroughly mixed.

A possible weakness in the performance of the trick is that if the shuffles are not controlled it is possible that the spectator in shuffling his or her packet will note and be suspicious of the face-up Aces in the packet. This weakness is over-come by the handling suggested for the trick ensuring that for all the shuffles the face-up Aces will always be in the performer's packet and that the Aces in the spectator's packet will always be face-down.

"Magic Clocks"

Versions of this effect can be found in many books on card magic. Karl Fulves describes one version, *"Crazy Clocks"* at pages 14-16 in his book *"More Self-Working Card Magic"* (Dover, New York, 1984). It depends for its working on the performer knowing the identity of the 13th card down from the top of the pack. Knowing this card the performer is in a position to predict that it will be this card that will eventually be chosen by the spectator. To produce this outcome the performer begins by inviting the spectator to think of any hour on a clock face. The spectator then secretly removes from the top of the pack the number of cards corresponding to the hour he or she has selected and hides them away. The performer then deals out into a face-down pile on the table the top 12 cards of the pack and then takes these cards and deals them out face-up to form the face of the clock. The spectator is then invited to declare his or her chosen hour and to note the card at that hour on the clock face. It will be the card predicted by the performer.

Fulves strengthens the presentation of the trick by suggesting that the performer should write his or her prediction on a slip of paper which is handed to the spectator at the beginning of the performance, and by also writing the selected hour on a second slip of paper once he or she has seen the position of the known card in the lay-out of the clock face. Additionally, Fulves notes that if the performer identifies not only the 13th card in the pack but also the 25th then he or she may place aside all the cards used in the first part of the trick to form the face of the clock, replace the spectator's cards on top of the pack, and repeat the trick using as the prediction the identity of this 25th card.

I had a number of reservations about the mechanics of the trick as described by Fulves. The first was the necessity for the performer to identify the 13th card in the pack, the second was the counting off of the cards by the spectator, the third was that in forming the clock face the cards were placed face-up, and the fourth was that to prepare for the forming of the clock face the order of the cards had to be reversed by dealing them out and then dealing them into a clock face.

In my version of the trick the performer is required to know the top card of the pack. This opens up the possibility of easily controlling the return of any selected card to that position or easily positioning any required card at that position. The problem then is how to use this top card in the clock effect. The solution I decided upon was to deal out a 12-card packet of cards from which the spectator could remove an unknown number of cards, leaving the original top card of the pack at the bottom of the cards not taken by the spectator. If these cards were then used as the top cards of a new 12-card packet then the position of the original top card of the pack in the clock face would be the number of cards cut off by the spectator, provided that the cards were dealt out in reverse order (thus the requirement to construct the clock face in an anti-clockwise direction beginning at 11 o'clock). Finally, the cards forming the clock face could be dealt out face-down. All that was then required was to disguise the mechanism of the trick by a sequence of false cuts and false mixes.

I also thought that the trick could be strengthened by using two clock faces simultaneously and thus involving two spectators.

The positioning of the Aces does involve a somewhat complicated handling technique but the resulting effect more than justifies this.

"Spell Them Out"

It has already been noted that the Aces can be arranged in such a way that, once they are appropriately positioned within the pack, they may be spelled out (*see the section on "Just Think of An Ace" earlier in this chapter.*) This trick, *"Spell Them Out"*, extends this effect to two packs and directly involves three spectators.

The trick depends for its success on the handling of the cards to position the Aces.

It might be thought that the suggested handling is over-complicated. However, if it is studied carefully and practised diligently, it will be found to be not as complicated or forbidding as it appears at first sight. In any case, my own view is that the effect achieved more than justifies the procedure required to produce it.

"More Aces"

The first part of this trick, ie. the position of the Aces as the top cards of each of the packets, is a variation of a trick described by Jean Hugard in his book *"The Royal Road To Card Magic"* (Dover, New York, 1999) under the title *"A Poker Player's Picnic"*. In Hugard's version the spectator is directed to take each pile of cards in turn and to transfer three cards from the top of the pile to the bottom of the pile and then to take the next three cards from the top of the pile and place one on top of each of the other piles. Provided the final pile started with the four Aces as its top cards it follows that all the piles will finish with an Ace as the top card.

My suggested finish for the trick is a series of top card forces.

The first is what is usually referred to as *"The X Force"* or *"The Cross Card Force"*. It depends for its success on there being a reasonable interval of time (filled with distraction) between the cut being made and the forced card being revealed. The second force is merely a variation of the same force using a little more finesse.

The third force is a variation on what is known as the *"Cut Deeper Force"* developed by Ed Balducci. In its original form it places the card to be forced from the top of the pack to a position as the first face-down card in the pack. This is achieved by inviting the spectator to take the face-down pack, to cut off about the top ¼ of the pack, to turn those cards over and to place them on top of the rest of the pack. He or she is then invited to cut off about the top ½ of the pack, to turn those cards over, and to place them on top of the pack. In my variation the card to be forced will, at the end of the procedure, still be the top face-down card of the packet.

The fourth force, although very simple in execution, is very deceptive in terms of outcome, particularly as there is a delay between the forcing of the card and its revelation.

"Everybody's Ace"

A classic trick in the armoury of the performer of card magic is "Everybody's Card". It requires the forcing of the same card onto as many spectators as the performer wishes to involve and then arranging for them all to realise simultaneously that they have all chosen the same card. It depends for its success on a series of forces—preferably a series in which each force is different from all those which precede it.

In the chapter "Old Wine In A New Bottle" I suggest that a bridged card should be used as the card to be forced. This simplifies the performance, but adapting the trick to force the same Ace onto each spectator requires a different technique and for "Everybody's Ace" I have described four forces that can be used. These, when combined with the initial locating of the Ace, produce the required outcome.

The first force requires the performer to place an Ace face-down at the top of the face-down pack. In some circumstances, particularly where the performer assesses that the spectators are not paying a great deal of attention to the handling of the pack, this can be done with very little subterfuge being required. However, there are a number of techniques that can be used to disguise the move and one of these is set out in detail at paragraph 2 of the description of the trick "Magic Clocks".

The second force is a variation of the "Cut Deeper Force" used in the previous trick "More Aces". It places the card to be forced from the top of the pack as the first face-down card in the pack. The third force is yet a further variation of the same force.

The fourth and final force appears to be yet another variation of that used in the trick *"Finding The Aces"*. In this case, however, the force is using a totally different mechanism to lead to the required card. It is, in fact, merely a complicated (and, therefore, a deceiving) way of placing on top of the card to be forced the same number of cards cut off by the spectator.

The successful forcing of a card has always been an essential skill in performing tricks with cards and from the very beginnings of card magic to the present day performers have been devising methods to achieve it.

Readers might be interested to know that in one of his books Theodore Annemann describes over two hundred techniques for forcing not only cards but also numbers, colours, names, coins, and a variety of other objects: *"202 Methods of Forcing"* (Davenport, London, 1994). The techniques range from the so-called *"Classic Force"*, the success of which depends purely upon the skill of the performer to coincide the position of the required card in a spread pack with the grasping fingers of the spectator's advancing hand, to methods that are mechanical and self-working—a number of which are, to say the least, bizarre. They do, however, all work!

"OLD WINE IN A NEW BOTTLE"

The Pre-Arranged Tricks

"Think of A Card—Spell Another"

The basis of this trick is *"Duo Spell"* in Karl Fulves's book *More Self-Working Card Tricks* (pages 126/7), which for its effect depends upon a procedure developed by Paul Swinford. The trick, as described by Fulves, begins with a pre-arranged (or "stacked") pack with two 8-card sequences on top of the pack: (QH, 6C, 2H, JS, 8S, KD, 3D, 4C and JD, 10C, AH, QC, 7S, 5D, 8D, 3S). These cards are delivered to two spectators by handing the first eight cards to the first spectator and the second eight cards to the second spectator. The cards are then displayed, without disturbing their order, and each spectator is invited to think of a card in the hand they have been shown other than the first and last card (ie. he or she can select from the middle six cards of the hand). The hands are then put together, placing the second hand on top of the first. The performer then carries out what Fulves calls "a reverse faro", that is the extraction from the combined packet of every alternate card. To do this the first card of the packet is out-jogged at the outer end about half the length of the card. This card, together with the second card underneath it, is taken into the other hand. The procedure is repeated through the packet, taking each pair in turn under the previous pairs removed and placing them in alignment so that when you have gone through the packet cards 1, 3, 5, 7, 9, 11, 13, 15 are out-jogged outwards and cards 2, 4, 6, 8, 10, 12, 14, 16 are out-jogged inwards. You now pull the two packets apart, place the *inward* out-jogged cards in order face-down on the table and show the *outward* out-jogged cards to the two spectators, keeping them in order. Each spectator is asked to say if they see their mentally selected card. The two packets are then put together on the following basis: if both spectators answer "yes" or both answer "no" the hand they have looked at goes face-down on top of the other hand; if one has answered "yes" and the other has answered "no" then the hand they have *not* looked at goes on top of the hand they have looked at. This whole procedure is repeated two more times. You then perform one more "reverse faro", giving the *outward* out-jogged cards face-down to the first spectator and the *inward* out-jogged cards to the second spectator. When the spectators spell out their thought-of cards, using the spelling system described in the instructions for the trick *"Think of A Card— Spell Another"* they will arrive at each other's card. My first amendment to the presentation of the trick was to move to a pre-arrangement of the cards that would allow for dealing the cards out to the spectators rather than handing them out in a block. My second was to deal out the cards in an apparently random order as directed by the spectators. I also, at the same time, expanded the pre-arrangement to allow the cards to be dealt out into four hands—any one of which could be paired with any other. My next concern with the opening section of the trick was the fact that the spectators' choice of card was restricted to the middle six cards of a hand of eight cards. The first and last cards of the hands are there not to be spelled out but as an essential element in the mechanism of the locating and spelling process, whereas the middle six cards of each hand form a spelling-out sequence running from ten to fifteen letters. It occurred to me, however, that if the first and last card of each hand could be spelled out in nine letters and sixteen letters respectively then they too could be spelled out in the spelling-out process. Two problems arise in attempting to produce this outcome: the first is that there are no cards with nine or sixteen letters that spell out in the way used in the trick, and the second is that even if there were such cards the mechanics of the trick would require two cards of nine letters and two of sixteen letters. To simplify matters the solution to both problems was to introduce identical *"Joker Card"*'s (nine letters) and *"The Invisible Card"*'s (sixteen letters) into all the hands. My next concerns were with the strange and suspicious handling of the cards involved in the series of four "reverse faros", and the fact that both spectators were directed to look for their cards in the same hand. What seemed to me much more natural and less suspicious was to order the cards in such a way that they could be dealt to the spectators who could then look for their card in the hand that had been dealt to them. The mechanics of the deals set out in the description of the trick *"Think of A Card—Spell Another"* allow this to be done, the deals actually ordering the cards as necessary. All that was then required was to reverse the formula given by Fulves to allow for the search for the thought-of cards to be made in both hands. Finally, if the performer used a bridged card and a sequence of false cuts and shuffles the ordering of the cards could be made to appear totally random.

"Shuffle-Spell"

Jean Hugard describes the trick *"The Shuffled Spelling Bee"* in his book *Encyclopaedia of Card Tricks* (page 57 Dover edition; page 79 Foulsham edition). It relies for its effect on the pre-arrangement of the two black suits of the pack (Clubs: 2, K, 10, Q, 7, 3, 4, 9, 5, A, 6, 8, J; Spades: 3, 8, 7, A, Q, 6, 4, 2, J, K, 10, 9, 5). The red cards of the pack are mixed in any order. The Club cards are then placed on top of the red cards and the Spades beneath the red cards. Finally, a Joker card is placed at the middle of the red cards. With the pack so arranged the pack is divided by taking out the Joker card and the two packets thus created are riffle shuffled into each other. Thus the two pre-arranged suits, although distributed throughout the pack, will remain in the same pre-arranged order, allowing them to be extracted in the order shown above. This order allows the cards turned over from the top of the face-down Spades packet to be spelled out using the Clubs packet using the spelling system described for the trick *"Shuffle Spell"*. My version of the trick provides a stack and handling that brings all four suits into play. Again the use of a bridged card and false shuffles and false cuts at appropriate occasions during the performance would re-inforce the impression that the cards were being indiscriminately mixed. If there is a weakness in my version of the trick it is that the open spread of the cards could allow a particularly observant spectator to see the pattern of cards in the sequences, but, given a quick spread, and the fact that the two sequences are mixed in reverse order, the chances of this happening are very small. In addition, the dealing and separating out of the cards would appear to unscramble any sequences.

The Any-Pack Tricks

"Miraskill Denied"

Karl Fulves in his book *More Self-Working Card Tricks* (page 7) attributes the invention of the trick *"Miraskil"* (*sic*) to Stewart James and sets out a version of it developed by himself and Joseph K. Schmidt. There are many other versions. For example, Martin Gardner in his *Mathematics, Magic, and Mystery* (page 13) describes what he calls the *"Stewart James Colour Prediction"*, involving the secret removal of four cards from a full pack of cards to achieve its effect. Arthur F. MacTier in his book *Card Concepts* (page 268/74) devotes a whole chapter to the principle involved and a variety of effects employing it, and Jean Hugard in his book *The Encyclopaedia of Card Tricks* (page 330/1 Dover edition; pages 373/4 Foulsham edition) also describes the trick, again involving the removal of four cards from the pack. In brief, the effect depends on the fact that if you take a pack or a packet of cards, shuffle it, and deal out the cards in pairs, then the like pairs (Red/Red or Black/Black) will be equal in number, or there will be no like pairs at all (although the probability of the latter occurring with a full pack is very low indeed). If you then take the same pack or packet and remove two cards of any one colour, shuffle the pack or packet, and deal out again, the deal will produce one more pair of the opposite colour to the cards you have taken out or a single pair of the colour you have not taken out (although again there is a very low probability with a full pack of producing no like pairs at all). My first intention was to develop the effect without the secret removal of cards from the pack. This was very easily achieved by dividing the pack into two equal packets and, after allowing a spectator a free choice of either of the two packets, inventing a subterfuge to allow the performer to count the cards of one colour in the other packet and thus be in a position to predict the difference in number in the pairs dealt out by the spectator from the other packet, or to predict that there would be an equal number of like pairs. However, I was not happy with either the presentation or the strength of the outcome. I then had the idea of using the discarded unlike pairs in some way to reverse the outcome of the dealing, ie. to deal out the whole pack, after it had been mixed and shuffled, without producing a single like pair—an almost impossible chance. To achieve this I turned to what is known as the Gilbreath stack. This is a pre-arrangement of the pack into a complete alternating colour sequence: Red-Black-Red-Black or Black-Red-Black-Red, etc. The stack is so named from Norman Gilbreath who observed that "if a (pack) of cards in the order of alternating cards is cut into two parts, with the bottom colours of the two parts (being) of opposite colours, and, the two parts are riffle shuffled together, then each successive pair of cards is composed of one red card and one black card" (quoted in Arthur F. MacTier's *Card Concepts* (page 160)). Obviously, if I could demonstrate to the spectator the almost certain probability of producing like pairs from a full pack and even a part pack and at the same time arrange to produce a Gilbreath stack in the discard pile, then if I took the discard pile and, after shuffling and mixing it, I produced not a single like pair in the dealing out, I had what I considered an impressive effect—thus *"Miraskill Denied"*.

"Can You Believe It?"

In the early 1940s Paul Curry developed an effect know as *"Out of This World"* which had as its outcome the separating out from a mixed face-down pack all the red cards into one packet and all the black cards into another. In his book *Self-Working Close-up Card Magic* Karl Fulves describes it as "a modern-day classic" (page 114) and sets out the workings of a trick producing the effect using a pre-arrangement of the pack, two mugs into which the cards are placed as their face-colour is guessed at by a spectator, and four labelled cardboard markers to order the cards in the mugs according to the guesses made by the spectator. The pre-arrangement consists of the 26 red cards of the pack being placed on top of the 26 black cards with some form of secret marking on the back of the card in 26th position to indicate the division of the colours and to facilitate the cutting of the pack at this point. Two of the cardboard markers (A and B) are labelled with the same colour on both sides (ie. A: Red/Red; B: Black/Black) while the other two markers (C and D) are labelled with one colour on one side and the other colour on the other side (ie. Red/Black). The trick begins with the marker A being placed in one mug and the marker C (with the opposite colour label to A towards the spectators) being placed in the other mug. A spectator is then invited to guess the colour of each face-down card as it is taken from the top of the face-down pack. The cards are placed (unseen) in front of the appropriately labelled marker (they are, of course, all red-faced cards). When the performer reaches the secret mark indicating the separation of the colours her or she invites a second spectator to guess the face colour of the remaining cards and, to separate that spectator's cards from the first spectator's cards, the performer places the cardboard marker D in the mug containing marker C with the label of marker D that faces the spectators showing the opposite colour to marker C. Marker D is placed in front of the cards already in the mug. Marker B is placed in the same way in the mug containing marker A. The performer then distributes the second spectator's cards into the mugs as appropriate, placing them in front of the markers (again unseen, but they are, of course, all black-faced cards). If the cards in the mug containing markers A and B are taken out, whichever way they are examined the sequences of red and black cards will correspond with the markers. The cards in the other mug are taken by the performer who spreads them face-up to show that they too correspond with the markers. To my mind there were two major weaknesses in this presentation. The first was that, although the two separate halves of the pack could be shuffled and cut, it was not possible at any point during the performance of the trick to display the cards face-up. The second was that for the trick to succeed the fact that the markers C and D had different colour labels back and front needed to be concealed both during and at the conclusion of the performance of the trick. Fulves suggests means to overcome these weaknesses, but weaknesses they remain nevertheless. Fortunately, Arthur F. MacTier in his book *Card Concepts* (pages 268/74) approaches the presentation of the effect in an entirely different way, using a Gilbreath stack as described in the previous section of this chapter on *"Miraskill Denied"*. As it was possible to finish that trick with the cards in a Gilbreath stack I was attracted to MacTier's method of using such a stack as the basis of an *"Out of This World"* effect. I therefore drew heavily on his presentation in the method of separating the cards, but the trick, to my mind, is strengthened by the handling and particularly by the revelation of the two selected cards out of place in the two colour sequences.

"Prime Cut Selection"

The trick is essentially a bottom card force, using what Arthur F. MacTier in his *Card Concepts* (page 55) refers to as the *"George Sands's Prime Number Principle"*. In the context of the trick *"Prime Cut Selection"* the principle could be summarised as that if you take a face-down packet of cards in which the total number of cards is a prime number and transfer from the top of the packet to the bottom a number of cards between 1 and the total number of cards in the packet, transferring the cards singly and turning over (ie. face-up) the last card being transferred, and if you repeat this procedure, using the same number, until only one card in the packet remains face-down, then that face-down card will be what was the bottom card of the packet. MacTier in discussing the principle and describing an effect using it gives credit to Peter Duffie for the development of a trick on which his own is based. This is performed with the cards face-up and involves the prediction by the performer of the card that will be left face-up at the conclusion of the trick. My version of the force and of the trick allows the cards to be used face-down and uses a card selected by a spectator as the revealed card.

"Divination"

Jean Hugard and Frederick Braué in *The Royal Road to Card Magic* (pages 136-8) describe a trick to which they give the title *"An Incomprehensible Divination"*. They refer to it as an "old war horse". The effect is based on placing Ace to 10 in that order on the top of a packet with a Joker card at the bottom of the packet. The packet is then given a Charlier Shuffle with the performer secretly sighting the top card of the packet after the shuffle. The value of this card (with the Joker card counting as 11) is used to provide the performer with a key number. This the performer produces by subtracting the value of the top card from 12. The performer then invites the spectator to think of any number between 1 and 10 and secretly to transfer one by one that number of cards from the top to the bottom of the packet. The performer takes the packet and cuts the card at his key number to the top of the packet. He or she then asks the spectator to state the number of cards moved and when the top card of the packet is turned over its value is this number. This card is turned face-down on the top of the packet giving the performer the means to calculate a new key number and to continue the trick. For this second phase of the trick the performer names a number (which is the key number) and invites the spectator to think of any number between 1 and 10 and again secretly to make the appropriate transfer of cards from the top to the bottom of the packet. When the performer makes the necessary transfer of cards the card at the top of the packet will be of the value of the number thought of by the spectator. Again, turning the card face-down on the top of the packet provides the performer with the means of calculating yet another key number and the trick may be continued. The Joker is provided in the stack in the event of any spectator attempting to subvert the trick by not moving any cards. In that case when the performer's cut is completed then the top card of the pack will be the Joker card. This is an excellent trick, but I felt that a totally different and equally strong effect could be achieved using the same principle. My idea was to use two sequences of Ace to King in place of the Ace to 10 and Joker card sequence used by Hugard and Braué. The first advantage of such an arrangement was that the card to be sighted to arrive at the key number could be the bottom card of the packet, and the second advantage was that if a card of any value was added to the key number then the card at that position in the packet would be equal in value to the card value added. I could therefore give the other 26 cards of the pack to the spectator and allow him or her to choose any card from those 26 and, by adding the value of that card to my key number, match his card with a card of the same value from my packet without any transfer of cards from top to bottom, ie. I could deal out cards from the top of my packet or count the cards off the top of the packet. Finally, if I declared my number by choosing an appropriately valued card from the spectator's packet before he or she chose the card then the effect would be even stronger. All that was required then was to conceal the ordering of my packet and the mechanism of the trick and this I decided could be effectively achieved by either false cuts or false shuffles and/or a riffle shuffle and/or the use of a bridged card.

"Certain Card Snap"

The development of this trick proceeded in such a strange way that it is worth describing at length. The initial inspiration was *"The Certain Card Trick"* developed by Percy Abbott and described by Jean Hugard and Frederick Braué in their *Expert Card Techniques* (pages 404/5). In studying the trick as they described it I had a number of reservations about its presentation. The original trick required that the pack be reduced to 48 cards to allow for the subsequent lay-out of the cards. It also required that the performer knew the identity of the bottom card in this 48 card packet. The spectator is asked to cut the packet and note the card below the cut. As he or she does so the performer estimates the number of cards that the spectator cut-off. Then begins what I felt was a very complicated method of identifying the noted card. You begin by dividing your estimate of the number of cards taken by 6. This will give you a number, or a number plus a remainder. You ignore the remainder and take the number as your key number. The spectator is now instructed to deal out (face-up) from the packet, which has been re-constituted by placing the cut-off cards back onto the top of the packet, six cards side by side, then another six cards below them, and so on until there are six rows of cards with each row containing eight cards. The spectator then declares in which row he or she sees the noted card and the performer can then secretly calculate the position in the row of the noted card using the following formula: Add your key number to the number of cards down the row in which you see your known card (ie. what was the bottom card of the packet): if the spectator has indicated that his noted card is in the same row as your noted card then it is in a position in that row equal to your calculation (if the number is over 8 subtract 8): if the spectator has indicated a row to the right (from your point of view) of the row with your known card in it the noted card is in the same position down in that row as your calculation (again if it is over 8 subtract 8): if the spectator has indicated a row to the left of your known card then the noted card is at a position in that row equal to your calculation plus 1 (again if this number is over 8 subtract 8). My first thought was to simplify the formula for locating the noted card, and my second was to devise a means of allowing the cards to be placed face-down. Hugard and Braué in their version had suggested that a face-down lay-out of the cards could be achieved by marking the known card in some way so it was a simple matter for me to conclude that I could use a bridged card in place of such a marked card. It also occurred to me that if my bridged card was at the bottom of the pack as dealt then the bridged card would always be the last card dealt, that the noted card would always be to its left or in the same row, and that the position of the noted card in its row would always be equal to the key number. I thus had my simplified formula and the cards could be dealt out face-down. I also noted that if my known card (ie. the bridged card) was in a fixed position (which it was) then the noted card was always in the same position in whichever row it was. Two possibilities arose from this. The first was that if I could restrict the spectator's choice of cards to six possible cards I could predict without any calculation the position in the row of any of those cards. The second was that it did not matter in what order those cards were placed they would still finish in that same position in one of the rows. After a number of trials exploring these possibilities it became clear that the ideal spread for the selection of cards was eight cards and that to guarantee a cut into these cards half the packet should be used. Then by dealing the reconstituted packet out into eight 6-card rows I could be sure that the noted card was at the second position down in whatever row it was—and the dealing out of the cards in six card sequences could deliver any card of that sequence to any row. I also noted that if the bottom half of the packet was used then the card noted in that half would be dealt out as the next to last card in whatever row it was dealt to, ie. the card noted in the top half would be one down from the top of the row it was dealt to and the card noted in the bottom half would be one up from the bottom of its row. Thus if one half was reversed in order a game of "Snap" would bring both cards together. This led me to the conclusion that I could involve two spectators, each choosing a card from a 24-card packet. After a number of trials along these lines I decided that I could guarantee a selection from the middle eight cards of a 24-card packet by dealing out six 8-card hands and allowing the spectators to choose any card in any hand. This also meant that I could allow the spectators to shuffle all the hands both before and after selection. All this, of course, was taking me further and further away from Abbott's original trick, but I felt that the outcome was equally, if not more, mystifying and striking.

"Think of An Ace"

As noted earlier in this chapter, this trick depends for its effect on the fortunate fact that the number of letters in spelling out the Aces can be manipulated to produce a sequence: AC (10), AH (11), AD (13). Thus any one of them can be spelled out by taking the card placed at the appropriate position in the pack. AS (11) is accommodated into the sequence by placing it between AH (11) and AD (13) and by taking the card left on top of the packet, ie. the 12th card.

"A Magic Number"

In his *Mathematics, Magic, and Mystery* (pages 7/8) Martin Gardner describes a trick with the title *"A Baffling Prediction"* in which a spectator chooses four cards from any twelve cards from the pack. The eight cards not chosen are returned to the bottom of the pack. The performer then takes each of the chosen cards in turn and deals out onto each card the number of cards required to bring the total to 10 (ie. on a 3 the performer would deal seven cards), the picture or court cards counting as 10s receive no cards. The spectator now totals the values of the original four cards he or she chose and counts down the remainder of the pack to the card at this number which will be what was the bottom card of the pack at the very start of the trick and which the performer could therefore have predicted. Gardner follows this with a description of the improvement made to this trick by Henry Christ which takes it to a different level. In this version the spectator selects any card from any nine cards from the pack. He or she places the selected card on top of the cards not selected and the remainder of the pack on top of this packet. The trick then proceeds as I have described for the trick *"A Magic Number"*. My own version uses eight cards from the pack from which the spectator may select his or her card. This is to allow for the use of the bridged card, and the use of false cuts and false shuffles to obscure the ordering of the pack. Obviously, the "secret" of the trick is the positioning of the selected card as the 9th card from the bottom of the pack. The mathematical principle involved is illustrated below:

Basic Trick

Value of First Card	3 6 8 2 = 19
No. of Cards Placed	7 4 2 8
Total No. of Cards Used	8 5 3 9 = 25
52 − 25 = 27 − 19 = 8	
Value of First Card	8 K(10) 2 A = 21
No. of Cards Placed	2 − 8 9
Total No. of Cards Used	3 1 9 10 = 23
52 − 23 = 29 − 21 = 8	

Henry Christ's Variation

Value of Coincident Card	2 5 − 6 = 13
No. of Cards Placed	9 6 11 5 = 31
52 − 31 = 21 − 13 = 8	
Value of Coincident Card	6 8 2 1 = 17
No. of Cards Placed	5 3 9 10 = 27
52 − 27 = 25 − 17 = 8	

"Real Magic"

This trick developed from studying the trick *"The Magic of Manhattan"* described by Martin Gardner in his *Mathematics, Magic, and Mystery* (pages 20/1). In that trick the cards are cut near the centre of the pack by a spectator, who then takes either packet, counts the cards in it, and notes the card at the position from the bottom of the packet which is indicated by adding together the digits of the number of cards in the packet. The spectator then places the packet on top of the other packet to reconstitute the pack. Using this procedure the noted card will always be at the 19th position from the top of the pack so that if the performer then spells out the phrase *"The Magic of Manhattan"* or any other nineteen letter phrase he or she will arrive at the noted card. It occurred to me that the effect could be strengthened by allowing the spectator to cut off any number of cards above 10 and then by adjusting the order of the cut-off cards and controlling their position in the re-constituted pack it would be possible, using one of four suitable phrases, to arrive at the noted card. This version also allows all the counting, including that by the spectator, to be done from the top of the pack and the packet, which is a much more natural procedure than counting up from the bottom of the packet as in the original trick.

The Two-Pack Trick

"Nobody Knows Anything"

. The effect is achieved by an adaptation of the *"Shuffle-Bored"* principle developed by Simon Aronson (*Bound to Please*, pages 145-71) and also discussed by Arthur F. MacTier in his *Card Concepts* (pages 100-06). In essence the principle is that if a pack of cards is divided into two packets and if a number of cards from each packet are turned over and shuffled into the other packet and this process is repeated as many times as wished, then, if, finally, one of the packets is turned over and shuffled into the other packet, the pack will contain the original two packets, one face-up and the other face-down. Some years earlier Bob Hummer had noted a very similar effect based on the fact that if a face-down packet containing an even number of cards was taken and the top two cards were turned face-up and the pack then cut and completed, and this process was repeated as many times as wished then if every other card in the packet was turned over the number of face-up cards in the packet would be half the total number of cards in the packet (see MacTier's *Card Concepts*, page 107 and Gardner's *Mathematics, Magic, and Mystery*, pages 17/19). For the trick *"Nobody Knows Anything"* I have used two packs of cards and a sequence of riffle shuffles to add to the "confusion". The use of the bridged card allows the division of the pack for these shuffles to be controlled.

The Final Tricks

"Same Number—Same Card"

In his book *Card Concepts* (pages 34/36) Arthur F. MacTier sets out and discusses two "principles" involving counting sequences using packs of cards. The first was developed by Martin D. Kruskel and the second came from an effect developed by Alexander F. Kraus. The former is based on the fact that if you take a pack of cards and turn over the first card at the top of the pack and then go to the card at the position in the pack indicated by the value of the first card and turn that card over, take the value of that card as a new starting point and go through the pack repeating this process, you will eventually arrive at the last card in the pack or at a card with a value greater than the number of the cards left in the pack. If this card is noted and the whole process is repeated, again and again, using the second card of the pack as the starting point, then the third, then the fourth, etc. there is a fair probability that you will finish the sequence on the same card. In fact, the probability is the probability of the sequencing coinciding at some point. This probability can be significantly increased by a number of subterfuges, eg. by counting the picture or court cards as 10s, or, even better, as 1s. MacTier then describes a very elegant and striking effect using this principle. It uses two packs of cards. In essence the trick consists of the spectator and the performer each thinking of a number from 1 to 10 and using that number as the starting point of the process described above for their own pack. The packs are then exchanged, the order of the packs not being disturbed. The spectator and the performer then go through the counting process again, this time using their own thought-of number as the starting point. Each should arrive at the other's card. Although the probability of success is quite high it is still only a probability, and MacTier considers it prudent to provide a means of disguising failure. However, the second principle can have a guaranteed outcome in that if a sequence of cards from King through to Ace is placed on the bottom of a pack and if a card is taken from near the top of the pack and used as the first card in the counting process then the total of the turned-up cards will always be 52. Moreover, the cards above the stack may be shuffled on each count and there is no requirement to adjust the values of the high value cards thus they can be given their actual values: J (11), Q (12), K (13). It occurred to me that the two "principles" could be combined to use the guaranteed outcome of the second "principle" to disguise the fact that the first "principle" had not led to a successful outcome. In fact, given that the totalling effect would work every time, there was a fair probability that the "each participant finds the other's card" would work and a very fair probability that one of the cards would be arrived at in the counting-out process. However, there are further variations of the second "principle" from which it is possible to develop other effects with a guaranteed outcome. The first variation I tried was of retaining the King to Ace stack at the bottom of the pack and cutting a number of cards from the top of the pack. Thus, when you have completed the counting out process described above the number of cards cut off would be equal to 52 minus the total arrived at by the counting process. For example, if you could secretly remove say five cards from the pack before the counting out began then you could predict that the total arrived at would be 47 (52 - 5). Alternatively, you could allow a spectator to select the starting point in the pack for the count (say, the 5th card down) and predict that the total arrived at would be 48 (52 - 5 = 47 + 1 = 48). If the selected starting point was the 15th card in the pack then the total arrived at would be 38 (52 - 15 = 37 plus 1 = 38). The second variation I tried was to place a King through Ace stack at the top of the pack and a King through Ace stack at the bottom of the pack. With this pre-arrangement it would be possible to predict that the total arrived at by the counting process would be 52 minus the selected number plus 1. You could also, if the count was repeated without disturbing the order of the pack, but with a different starting point, predict that the total arrived at would be 52 minus the second selected number plus 1, and that at the end of the second count you would arrive at the same card as on the first count. In fact, the second card in the counting process will always begin the same sequence irrespective of what number is selected as the starting point, ie. it will be the 14th card from the top of the pack. The third variation of this second "principle" arises from the observation that it can be applied to a packet of cards as well as to the whole pack. For example, if you remove from the pack the picture or court cards you will be left with a packet of 40 cards. If you then place a 10 through to Ace at the bottom of this packet and ask a spectator at what number card in the packet he or she wishes to begin the counting process, the total that will be arrived at will be 40 minus the number selected plus 1. If you repeat the process for another number, without disturbing the order of the packet, you will arrive at a different total number but one that you could have predicted immediately the spectator had chosen at what point in the packet he or she wished the counting process to start. All these variations had the potential to produce a strong effect but obviously there were many more variations hidden away behind the principle which had equal potential. I determined to try to find some of the them. After much experimentation I came to a number of conclusions. The first was that the stack at the top of the pack could be eliminated either by using a thought-of number or by using a card to which the spectator could assign any value. My second conclusion was that in the counting processes leading to an over-all total I could allow the spectator to choose any card in the packets counted out without affecting the eventual outcome of the total number: it was only when I wished to arrive at the same card in two counts that the cards needed to be kept in the same order within the packets. The third conclusion arose out of the need to disguise the placing of the stack at the bottom of the pack and I concluded that this could be achieved by misdirecting the attention of the spectator by asking him or her to sort though the cards in the pack extracting certain cards and that the most logical cards for the spectator to be searching for were the picture or court cards. This line of thought re-inforced my next conclusion that a number of cards less than the full pack produced a less suspicion-inducing total than the 52 produced by the full pack. It also reduced the stack from thirteen down to a more manageable ten cards. However, my most startling conclusion was that if the 10 to Ace sequence was placed *within* the pack then not only did it guarantee that the dealing would finish on the same card but it also guaranteed that the total arrived at would (if the order of the cards was not disturbed) always be the same irrespective of the starting number. A few moments thought shows why. After entry into the 10 to Ace sequence the subsequent cards will always be the same and thus have the same total number. The cards preceding the 10 to Ace sequence plus the card arrived at in the sequence will also have the same total number. Thus the two separate totals added together will always give the same overall total. It was out of these thoughts and conclusions that I eventually arrived at the trick *"Same Number—Same Card"*.

"Everybody Shouts"

As noted earlier in this chapter, this is a classic effect in card magic. It has been described and performed in many variations. In its basic form it is the forcing of the same card on a number of spectators and then revealing that card in a striking way to all of the spectators at the same time. It is usually known as *"Everybody's Card"*. Hugard and Braué describe a version of the trick suitable for performance before a theatre-sized audience involving two forces, and four sleights-of-hand to change the top card of the pack. Mercifully, they also describe the trick adapted for performance before a smaller audience that reduces the requirement for manipulation—but not by much (*The Royal Road to Card Magic*, pages 281/7). However, in his *Encyclopaedia of Card Tricks* (page 97 Dover Edition: page 109 Foulsham edition) Hugard reduces the handling requirement to forcing only, using what is known as a "slick" card, which is a card highly polished on its face so that it can be easily located in the pack. It is this version I have taken as the basis for *"Everybody Shouts"*, using the bridged card in place of the "slick" card. The use of the bridged card in this way enables the performer to allow the spectators to do what they will with the pack in the way of shuffles and cuts after they have placed the selected card back into the pack. There is a weakness in the requirement for each spectator to take either the top or bottom card of the pack as the selected card. This could be overcome by varying the forcing method used. However, my own preference is to keep the process as simple as possible. It is safer and still convincing to perform the trick as described.

"OUT OF THE BOX"

Arranging And Setting The Pack

It has already been noted that when the *"Bicycle Rider Back"* pack is removed from its carton, and the Jokers and extraneous cards removed, it is in the order Ace to King (Hearts), Ace to King (Clubs), King to Ace (Diamonds), King to Ace (Spades). Such an arrangement is known as a *"Rusduck Stay Stack"*; so called from the name of the card performer, John Russell Duck, who developed a variety of effects using it. What he noted was that if a pack of cards so arranged was cut into two equal packets and the two packets were perfectly inter-weaved either one or more times then the halves of the packs are always mirror images of each other in relation to the values and positioning of the cards. It follows therefore that if the original order of the pack is changed to Ace to King (Clubs), Ace to King (Hearts), King to Ace (Diamonds), King to Ace (Spades) then the outcome of this interweaving will be that the halves of the pack will be mirror images of each other in relation not only to the value and positioning of the cards but also in relation to the colour of the cards, ie, the Black "2s", the Red "9s" will match, etc. The arrangement of the pack as described in the relevant section of the chapter *"Out Of The Box"* organises the pack into the appropriate configuration to produce this outcome.

Ideally, the pack should then be set by what are known as *"faro"* shuffles, where the cards are divided into two equal packets and then perfectly inter-weaved into each other. The technique required to produce such a result is difficult and, except in the hands of a very experienced and adept performer, unreliable. There are, however, other means by which the same outcome may be produced. One is by dealing out the cards into two packets followed by placing one packet on the other. Another is by using what Jean Tamariz in his book "*Mnemonica*" terms the "*anti-faro*", which entails dealing out the cards into four piles followed by a pick-up in reverse order to the order of the dealing. A second such deal will distribute the colours more thoroughly while still maintaining a mirror image order. A third will arrange the pack in matching pairs in the sequence: Aces, Kings, "2s", Queens, "3s, Jacks, "4s", "10s", "5s", "9s", "6s", "8s", "7s". A fourth deal would restore the pack to its original order.

For the reader who wishes to attempt to master the faro shuffle it can be performed either on the table or in the hands off the table. For the former begin by splitting the pack into two equal packets and placing them inner end to inner end. In holding the packets the thumbs should be at about the middle of the back sides of the packets, the index fingers should rest on the top of the packets, the second and third fingers should be on the front sides of the packets at the outer corners, and the little fingers should be at the outer ends of the packets at the front corners. Raise the inner touching ends of the packets by pushing the two packets together and thus forming a convex bend in each packet. In performing this move ensure that the tips of the second, third and little fingers and the thumbs maintain contact with the table. Once the convex bend has been produced in the packets weave the two packets into each other by moving the packets against each other front to back and back to front. Do not force the cards into each other—rather allow the tension created by the bend in the packets to inter-weave the cards.

To perform the shuffle in the hands and off the table begin again with the two packets end to end. One packet is held with the hand palm down and the other with the palm up. The thumbs of each hand are at the middle of the back sides of the packets. The first three fingers of the palm-down hand are at the front sides of the packets and the little finger abuts against the middle of the outside edge. With the palm-up hand the second and third fingers are at the front side of the cards at the middle of the packet, the index finger is at the middle of the outside end, and the little finger is lightly touching the bottom of the packet. The two packets are then pushed together to produce a convex bend in each packet with tension between the two packets. Then using this tension allow the two packets to interweave. In doing so do not attempt to force the cards.

In both procedures some performers prefer to angle the packets so that the two inner corners at the back of the pack only are in contact. Then, the weave having been made at that point, the packets are brought together to allow the cards to be pushed together.

"Cards And Numbers"

As the cards are configured so that the two halves of the pack are mirror images of each other the requirement for the performer is to know the position of the card selected in the spectator's half in order to calculate the position of the matching card in his or her own packet. In the second part of the trick this is achieved by what is usually referred to as "The Principle of 9", which is a method of producing the number 9 from any number from 10 to 19. The "principle", which is described in more detail in the earlier section of this chapter on the background to the trick *"Finding The Aces"*, is that for any such number if the two digits of the number are added together to give a single digit number and if that number is then subtracted from the original two digit number the result will always be 9, eg:

$(10 = 1 + 0 = 1) (10 - 1 = 9)$
$(17 = 1 + 7 = 8) (17 - 8 = 9)$
$(19 = 1 + 9 = 10) (19 - 10 = 9)$

Because the routine set out in the chapter *"Out Of The Box"* requires that the order of the cards within the pack is preserved the handling for this trick ensures that the selected card will always be what is the 10th card down in the spectator's half of the face-down pack.

"Bluff—Double Bluff"

The reader will have noted from the comments on the setting of the pack given earlier in this chapter that a third dealing out of the cards from a Rusduck Stay Stack not only produces the two halves of the pack in mirror images but also produces mirror images of the cards by pairs. This trick, "Bluff—Double Bluff", takes advantages of this arrangement, which has been arrived at by the second dealing out in the previous trick "Cards And Numbers". All that is then required to arrange the cards for the successful outcome of "Bluff—Double Bluff" is to reverse the order of the spectator's half of the pack.

Separating The Cards

The outcome of this trick derives from the observation by Norman Gilbreath (already noted in the discussion of the trick *"Miraskill Denied"* earlier in this chapter) that if a pack of cards, where the cards are distributed throughout the pack in alternating colours, is cut so that the bottom cards of the two packets are of different colours, then, if the two packets are riffle shuffled together and the cards dealt out in pairs, each pair will contain a card of each colour. The order in which the colours occur cannot be predicted, but there will always be one card of each colour.

For a full discussion of the principles arising from this observation and the variety of uses to which they may be put in card magic the reader is referred to Arthur F. MacTier's book *"Card Concepts"*.

"All In Order"

This trick combines the principal feature of the Charlier Shuffle with that of the riffle shuffle.

The Charlier Shuffle (named after the French card performer who developed it) ensures that the cards, although apparently randomly mixed, remain in the order that would have resulted had the cards been merely cut and completed. Thus the cards can be restored to their original order by handling that returns what was the bottom card back to that position. The reader might be interested to note that Jean Hugard in his book *"The Royal Road To Card Magic"* observed that of all the false shuffles that there are "for . . . laymen (the Charlier Shuffle) is the most convincing false shuffle extant," and the beginner in card magic might be pleased to know that he also observes that the shuffle is "most effective when done rather clumsily".

The riffle shuffle ensures that when two packets of cards are riffle shuffled together, although the packets are mixed together, the original order of each packet remains the same. Readers who would be interested to see the various effects that can be produced using the shuffle should see the chapter *"Riffle-Shuffle Setups"* in Karl Fulves' book *"More Self-Working Card Tricks"*.

"Same Number—Same Card"

This trick is used in both the *"Out Of The Box"* routine and the *"Old Wine In A New Bottle"* routine. The background to this trick is fully discussed in an earlier section of this chapter.

"The Next Turn"

This is a very straight-forward trick which depends for its outcome on disturbing the order of a sequence of cards. The secret of success with the trick is the ability to recognise the break of sequence which on occasions can be complicated. There is, however, a fool-proof system for verifying the out-of-sequence card. Take, for example, the sequence "3" – "2" – "Q" – "A" – "K" – "J" – "10" – "9" – "8" – "7" – "6" – "5" – "4". Begin with the Ace (A) and go either right or left to pick up the sequence "2" – "3" – "4" etc., ignoring any intervening cards. The card that is missing from and out of the sequence before you arrive back at the Ace is the selected card. In this example "Q" is the selected card.

Here are some further examples (the selected card is printed **bold**):

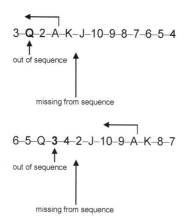

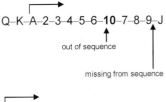

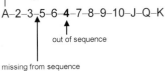

This trick is brought to a conclusion with what is know as "The Circus Trick", so called from its use by card-sharpers at fairs and circuses who gulled a spectator into making what he or she thought was a certain winning bet by offering to wager that "the next card turned over will be your selected card" when the spectator had already seen the selected card dealt out onto the table.

"You Can Find It"

It has already been observed in the *"Introduction"* that "it is surprising what can go unnoticed provided it is done boldly and the attention of the spectators distracted by directing it elsewhere". This trick has a number of examples of the very effective use of this technique to divert the attention of the spectator away from the handling of the cards by the performer.

At paragraph 7 of the description of the trick the spectator cuts the bottom half of the pack into two roughly equal packets. He or she is then involved in searching through the other half of the pack. This provides the performer with the ideal opportunity to arrange the cut-off cards in what is usually referred to as a false "cross cut" by placing the bottom packet of the cut on the packet that has been cut off, the top card of which is the card required by the performer. The deception is enhanced by the delay produced by the searching before the attention of the spectator is drawn back to the cut.

Another example can be found in the procedure for cutting the cards at paragraph 10 (1) of the description of the trick where again the requirement of the spectator to search for and count particular cards allows the performer to locate the required cards in the pack.

ARRANGING A STACK FOR SPELLING OR DEALING

T HERE ARE A NUMBER of tricks described in this book that require the pre-arrangement of the pack or packet to allow the cards to be spelled out. Others require the placing of a pre-ordered stack in the pack, arranged in such a way that it can be dealt out. On the assumption that it might be of interest and use to the reader some methods that can be used to do this are described in this section.

Spelling Arrangements

Hugard in his *Encyclopaedia of Card Tricks* (page 41, Dover edition: page 61, Foulsham edition) describes a method of arranging a packet of cards in such a way that the cards from Ace through to King can be spelled out by taking a card in turn for each letter of the spelling from the top of the face-down packet, transferring these cards face-down in turn to the bottom of the packet and turning over the card then at the top of the packet to reveal the spelled-out card. This card is then removed from the packet and placed on the table. The procedure begins by marking out on a sheet of paper thirteen spaces and then moving along the spaces from left to right spelling out the letters of A – C – E. You then enter A in the next space and continue on from the space after the one you have filled, spelling out T – W – O and entering 2 in the next space. You continue in this way, always moving from left to right and skipping over any occupied space, until you have filled all the spaces. You will find that at the end of the process you will finish with an order of cards 3 – 8 – 7 – A – Q – 6 – 4 – 2 – J – K – 10 – 9 – 5 and you will find that from this order you are able to spell out all the cards from Ace to King using the spelling system described above.

The system can be adapted to spell out any sequence. For example, to spell out 4, 8, 3, and King in that order from a 9-card packet begin by marking out the nine spaces. After spelling out F – O – U – R place the figure 4 in the next space. If you then go to the next space and spell out E – I – G – H – T you will place the figure 8 in the 2ⁿᵈ space, and, following the same procedure, you will spell out T –

H – R – E – E and place the figure 3 in the last space, and after spelling out K – I – N – G you will place the letter K in the 7th space. The stack you require therefore is X – 8 – X – X – 4 – X – K – X – 3 (where X is any card).

An alternative method of achieving the same end using the cards themselves to determine the necessary ordering can be used. To do this begin by taking a sequence of cards from Ace through to King and placing them face-up on the table with Ace at the left end of the row and King at the right end of the row. Now spell out A – C – E beginning at the left end of the row and moving along the cards counting a letter on each card. When you have reached the end, pick up the card immediately to its right (which will be the 4), take the Ace from its position at the beginning of the row and place it face-down at the position vacated by the 4. Now place the 4 face-up at the position vacated by the Ace. Starting with the first face-up card after the face-down Ace count out T – W – O, pick up the next card (which will be the 8), take the 2 from its position and place it face-down at the position vacated by the 8 and place the 8 face-up in the position vacated by the 2. Now, starting with the first face-up card after the face-down 2 spell out T – H – R – E – E, counting along the row. This will bring you to the end of the row so the first face-up card is at the beginning of the row (it is, of course, the 4). Pick up the 4, take the 3 from its position and place it face-down at the position vacated by the 4 and place the 4 face-up at the position vacated by the 3. Now, starting with the first face-up card after the face-down 3, spell and count out F – O – U – R (ignoring any face-down card in the counting out), take the next face-up card (which will be the 7) and transpose it with the 4, placing the 7 face-up and the 4 face-down. Continue with this spelling and counting and, when necessary, transposing procedure, ignoring any face-down cards, until all the cards but the

King are face-down. (You will find that the final positions of the 6, 7, and 8 do not require any transposition.) If you then turn the cards face-up along the row you will see that you have arrived at the arrangement required.

Dealing Arrangements

For the purpose of illustration a worst case scenario will be assumed and that is that you wish to deal out face-down from a face-down pack two 26-card piles which, after they have been examined, will have the second pile placed on top of the first. You then wish to deal out from the reconstituted pack four 13-card hands, each in a particular order, ie. Hearts, Clubs, Diamonds, Spades in that order, each with Ace to King with Ace as the top card of each face down hand. All deals to be consecutive dealing, ie. a card in turn to each hand or pile. The following tables are the basis on which the required organisation of the cards can be determined.

Hands required

Hand 1: (Top):	1 – 2 – 3 – 4 – 5 – 6 – 7 – 8 – 9 – 10 – 11 – 12 – 13
Hand 2: (Top):	14 – 15 – 16 – 17 – 18 – 19 – 20 – 21 – 22 – 23 – 24 – 25 – 26
Hand 3: (Top):	27 – 28 – 29 – 30 – 31 – 32 – 33 – 34 – 35 – 36 – 37 – 38 – 39
Hand 4: (Top):	40 – 41 – 42 – 43 – 44 – 45 – 46 – 47 – 48 – 49 – 50 – 51 – 52

Pack Required for Dealing (Face-down)

(Top):	13 – 26 – 39 – 52 // 12 – 25 – 38 – 51 // 11 – 24 – 37 – 50 // 10 – 23 – 36 – 49 // 9 – 22 – 35 – 48 // 8 – 21 – 34 – 47 // 7 – 20 – **33 – 46** // 6 – **19 – 32 – 45** // 5 – **18 – 31 – 44** // 4 – **17 – 30 – 43** // 3 – **16 – 29 – 42** // 2 – **15 – 28 – 41** // 1 – **14 – 27 – 40**

Required Two Pile Deal (Face-down)

(Pile B to be placed on Pile A to re-constitute pack)

Hand A: (Top):	**33 – 46 – 6 – 19 – 32 – 45 – 5 – 18 – 31 – 44 – 4 – 17 – 30 – 43 – 3 – 16 – 29 – 42 – 2 – 15 – 28 – 41 – 1 – 14 – 27 – 40**
Hand B: (Top):	13 – 26 – 39 – 52 – 12 – 25 – 38 – 51 – 11 – 24 – 37 – 50 – 10 – 23 – 36 – 49 – 9 – 22 – 35 – 48 – 8 – 21 – 34 – 47 – 7 – 20

Pack Required to Deal Two Piles (Face-down)

(Top):	40 – 20 – 27 – 7 – 14 – 47 – 1 – 34 – 41
	21 – 28 – 8 – 15 – 48 – 2 – 35 – 42
	22 – 29 – 9 – 16 – 49 – 3 – 36 – 43
	23 – 30 – 10 – 17 – 50 – 4 – 37 – 44
	24 – 31 – 11 – 18 – 51 – 5 – 38 – 45
	25 – 32 – 12 – 19 – 52 – 6 – 39 – 46
	26 – 33 – 13

Applied to Four-Hand Deal to Give Ace to King Sequence in Hearts, Clubs, Diamonds, Spades in That Order, Through A Two Pile Deal

1	2	3	4	5	6	7	8	9	10	11	12	13
AH	2H	3H	4H	5H	6H	7H	8H	9H	10H	JH	QH	KH

14	15	16	17	18	19	20	21	22	23	24	25	26
AC	2C	3C	4C	5C	6C	7C	8C	9C	10C	JC	QC	KC

27	28	29	30	31	32	33	34	35	36	37	38	39
AD	2D	3D	4D	5D	6D	7D	8D	9D	10D	JD	QD	KD

40	41	42	43	44	45	46	47	48	49	50	51	52
AS	2S	3S	4S	5S	6S	7S	8S	9S	10S	JS	QS	KS

Required Pack (Face-down)

(Top):	AS – 7C – AD – 7H – AC – 8S – AH – 8 D
	– 2S – 8C – 2D – 8H – 2C – 9S – 2H – 9 D
	– 3S – 9C – 3D – 9H – 3C – 10S – 3H –10D
	– 4S –10C – 4D –10H – 4C – JS – 4H – J D
	– 5S – JC – 5D – JH – 5C – QS – 5H –Q D
	– 6S – QC – 6D – QH – 6C – KS – 6H – K D
	– 7S – KC – 7D – KH

The example illustrates the process. Any required hands can be produced by substituting the identities of the required cards as appropriate and by adjusting the numbers in the tables to correspond with the number of cards in use.